SOCIALISM AND BUREAUCRACY

ANDRAS HEGEDUS

Socialism and Bureaucracy

ALLISON & BUSBY, LONDON

First published in Great Britain 1976
by Allison and Busby Limited
6a Noel Street, London W1V 3RB

Copyright © Andras Hegedus 1976
Translation copyright © Allison & Busby 1976
Hardback ISBN 0 85031 178 0
Paperback ISBN 0 85031 179 9

Set in 10pt Times and printed by
Villiers Publications Ltd, Ingestre Road, London NW5 1UL

Contents

Editor's Note

The majority of the essays in this volume are chapters taken from a larger work by Andras Hegedus which is unpublished in Hungarian or English, and is likely to remain so in the foreseeable future; the rest of the essays outline other ideas which went into the same work. All the individual chapters of the present work have appeared in various journals in Hungary and are presented here in chronological order of their publication, which enables us to trace the development of the ideas through the influence of the circumstances in which they were set down, most notably the Hungarian economic reform and the events of the late sixties in East European society.

The sources and dates of the essays in this volume are as follows:

Marx's analysis of bureaucracy (*Magyar Tudomany*, 1966, no. 4)

Historical antecedents of the fight against bureaucracy (*Kortars*, 1966, no. 8)

Economic management and social control (*Kozgazdasagi Szemle*, 1966, no. 7-8)

Scientific research and the management apparatus (*Magyar Tudomany*, 1967, no. 8)

Alternatives of social development (*Kortars*, 1968, no. 6)

The relevance of the "trade union debate" (*Uj Iras*, 1968, no. 12)

Towards a sociological analysis of property relations (*Magyar Filozofiai Szemle*, 1969, no. 6)

Lenin and the alternative types of socialist economy (*Kozgazdasagi Szemle*, 1970, no. 4)

Economic reform and the basic types of socialist economic system (*Kozgazdasagi Szemle*, 1970, no. 5)

Bureaucratism and the social pathology of the administration (*Kortars*, 1970, no. 7).

The intelligentsia and the administration (*Forras*, 1970, no. 5)

The publishers wish to thank those who helped to supervise and edit the translation, and who advised in various capacities.

I: Marx's Analysis of Bureaucracy

There are significant differences between the popular and the scientific definitions of bureaucracy. In common parlance, the term implies the insolence of office, administrative delays and red tape, the fear of making decisions, and so on. Scientific explanations of bureaucracy, on the other hand (which, as I shall try to show, were first attempted by Marx), try to examine the relationship of the administrative and managerial apparatus to the specific social context in which it arose and to define that relationship in terms of a larger conceptual framework. Many sociologists today tend to diverge from Marx's interpretation and treat bureaucracy as the blundering of incompetent officials rather than as a set of substantive relations to which certain types of socio-economic administration or management give rise. If this were really so, then the problem of bureaucracy could be solved simply by replacing a few incompetent officials.

It is no exaggeration to say that without a proper and more explicit sociological interpretation of bureaucracy and without an understanding of the essential nature of bureaucratic relationships, as they develop both within the administrative framework and between the administration and society as a whole, it is impossible to form a true picture of different societies as they really are.

Historically, bureaucracy made its appearance at a specific point in the development of the division of labour, when the functions of enforcing property and ownership rights began to be performed separately from those relating to the administration of society. This was a necessary result of objective circumstances, of an impulse from both the proprietors and the direct producers (the principal social classes), which occurred when the integration of society reached the point at which a hierarchic, specialised and functionally skilled organisation became necessary for the performance of administrative functions. In this intricate social process, the decisive factor was that the proprietor—whether an individual or a social community—was no longer able to perform directly the management functions which derived from the fact of his ownership, and he was thus forced to share his power with a hierarchically and professionally organised social group qualified to perform these tasks. This group became, however, not only the executor of

9

specific management functions but simultaneously acquired specific interests of its own.

Initially, the need to delegate administrative functions arose because there were certain tasks, such as irrigation and flood control, which exceeded the capabilities of smaller communities and which required special skills and, consequently, greater control and stability in management—even though the need was not evident in terms of the level of development of the division of labour. Bureaucracies of this type already existed in ancient societies and often acquired important powers—as for example in Egypt, where the priests of Amon strove, not without success, to take effective possession of land, slaves and accumulated treasure. Bureaucracy also played an outstanding role in countries where the Asiatic mode of production prevailed; they were in large part characterised by the dominance of bureaucratic conditions. Here, efforts aimed at centralisation were supported above all by bureaucratic officials and the aristocracy, and the bureaucracy played a leading part in bringing communal property under the ownership of the patriarchal state.

At a later date, the development of a market economy and conditions of capitalist ownership was accompanied by a process of national integration and the formation of the nation-state, or of societies which included several nationals within the framework of a single state or federation of states. To control an extensive commodity trade, the creation of a hierarchical, relatively stable and skilled administrative apparatus at both the national and the state level was required. The resulting stratum served, at the outset, the ruling sovereigns of the enlightened monarchies, but indirectly it served the rising new class of the bourgeoisie.

This development was well described by Marx, who noted that "the privileges of landowners and the franchises of the towns had changed into different attributes of state power, feudal dignitaries into salaried officials and the variegated medieval plenipotentiaries who, in that time, had opposed each other, into the regulated scheme of a state power the activity of which was distributed and centralised as in factories".[1]

This bureaucracy was still an integral part of the ruling class, but in a different way than it had been in slave societies or in countries characterised by the Asiatic mode of production. It possessed, to a greater extent, independent and particularised interests; it was subordinated to the ruling class only through the intermediary of a variety of intricate mechanisms; and it served, even though indirectly, the emerging class of the bourgeoisie.

10

For the first time in history, the way was open for the bureaucracy to become a genuinely independent socio-political force, for its establishment had been dictated by general economic conditions and not in answer to specific and immediate economic or geographic needs.

The bureaucracy as a vehicle of substantive social relations

Whatever its particular form, bureaucracy has always been the possessor of power conferred by others; the shadow power of history, this social stratum has acted only on the behalf of another power. Thus, Amon acted for the Pharaoh, the emperor of China embodied the patriarchal state, while the king of France held his office by the grace of God. Nor was the situation different under fully developed capitalism, even though it became much more complicated: the administration was separated from both the property-owning class and the direct producers, but it represented capitalism nonetheless.

What was the origin of the ever-increasing power of the bureaucracy under the enlightened monarchies? The question was first asked of French and English history, but the first person to answer it in accordance with the social and historical facts was Marx.

Even in the works of Hegel, bureaucracy was not treated as a social group with distinctive characteristics: officials and functionaries were only mentioned as those who acted on behalf of the enlightened ruler, or later, on behalf of the constitutional monarchy, the "state of reason". The organs of state administration and their officials acted as the representatives of some "higher" interest, as functionaries of the absolute or constitutional state who had no separate interests or aims of their own.

The young Marx was the first to bring to light the substantive characteristics of this state administration: that it was a distinct and separate social stratum with specific, particular interests, that it constituted the source of a set of distinctive, "bureaucratic" relationships, and finally, that it was not "civic life" which was held together by the state, but on the contrary, the state which was held together by "civic life".

Contemporary bourgeois sociologists usually trace the scientific treatment of bureaucracy no further back than Max Weber and fail to take into consideration the important theoretical conclusions reached by Marx. Nor was this helped by a dogmatic tendency long prevalent in marxism to treat Marx's writings on bureaucracy

11

as belonging to the activity of his youth and not as an integral part of his life-work.

Marx contested and refuted the voluntarist illusions of the young hegelian movement, which held that errors committed by the constitutional monarchical state could be eliminated or corrected through rational argument. Thus, the problem of bureaucracy played a very important role in the development of marxian sociological theory—in fact, it would not be far off the mark to say that this question was one of the most important factors in its development.

According to the young hegelians, the Prussian state could eventually develop into the "state of reason". Even if they were aware of the elaborate contradictions involved, they did not attribute this to the existence of substantive social relationships. Some hegelians shed their illusions on this point, but the majority were afraid of drawing the logical conclusions and continued to adhere to their belief that everything bad and "irrational" in the state could be corrected through the use of reason.

Marx was the first to lift the last veil of this illusion. He demonstrated that *certain mechanisms had developed within the state which were inseparable from it and which proved resistant to all rational argumentation, and that consequently, well-meaning and indulgent criticism was quite senseless*. Marx came to this realisation through the misery he observed when visiting the Moselle district as a newspaper reporter. His comparison of the hegelian theory of the state with the reality he saw led him to express a thought which is crucial to an understanding of the essential nature of bureaucracy:

"Due to its bureaucratic essence, administration was *unable* to grasp the reasons for the misery in the sphere of administration and could only see the reasons in the spheres of nature and private citizens, outside of the sphere of administration. Even with the best of intentions, devout humanism and the utmost intelligence, the administrative authorities were unable to do more than solve instantaneous and transitory conflicts and were incapable of eliminating the permanent conflicts between reality and principles of administration, partly because such measures or activities were not included in the tasks of their positions and partly because even the best intentions were bound to fail in breaking through a *substantive relation* or, in other words, destiny. *This substantive relationship was the bureaucratic relation*, both within the body of administration and in respect of the body managed."[2]

12

Marx's succinct and lucid comments need no further elucidation, but for the purposes of the ensuing discussion, the reader's attention should be drawn to one point. This is the mention of the two elements inherent in the existence of the bureaucracy: *bureaucratic relations within the administration and the relations of bureaucracy to the object of administration.* From this idea, it is only one step to showing the social and historical roots of bureaucracy and to the analysis of bureaucracy as a social group which is the source of these particular relationships and which, at the same time, is possessed of its own particular interests.

The young Marx initially accepted Hegel's concept of the official as one who represents general interests, but later, his analysis of the real relations involved led him to change his mind radically. Marx showed that special interests, with their roots in social conditions, developed objectively within the étatist type of administration characteristic of the constitutional monarchy.

To make clear the essential features of bureaucratic relationships, it had first to be shown that the administrative apparatus of the state, having separated naturally from society as a whole at a certain point in the development of the division of labour, acted as the representative of particular interests, rather than of the general interests of society and, because of this, strongly resisted the realisation of the true interests of society.

In his analysis of the feudal-capitalist state, as seen under Prussian conditions, which is contained in the *Critique of Hegel's "Philosophy of Law"*, Marx had already stated that "the real objective of the state . . . appeared in bureaucracy as an anti-state objective," and that "the spirit of bureaucracy was the 'formal spirit of state' ".

Thus bureaucracy made the "formal spirit of state" is that, the real spiritless character of the state, a categorical imperative. *Bureaucracy in itself becomes the final objective of the state.* Having made the content of bureaucracy its "formal" objective, it came everywhere into conflict with its "real" objectives and bureaucracy was forced to put forward its formal objectives as content and its real content as formal objectives. In conclusion, Marx states: "In bureaucracy, the identity of state interests and particular private objectives is formulated in such a way that state interests become a particular, private objective, in opposition to other private objectives."[8]

Marx considered this type of bureaucracy a social stratum with both power objectives and effective means of power at its disposal. In Prussia, he wrote in a paper published in 1848, "a perfectly organised bureaucratic hierarchy had reigned for forty years in public administration and the army", and he further stated that in Germany, this bureaucracy had been the arch-enemy of the 1848 bourgeois-democratic revolution.

Marx further emphasised the self-contained, independent power of the bureaucracy in his paper *Moralising Critique and Critical Morals*. He wrote that the hands of the ruling princes in the absolutist Prussian state had been bound not only by their own personal prejudices, but by the bourgeois, military and clerical bureaucracy "which had been absolutely unwilling to give up its ruling positions to enter into the service of the bourgeoisie".

Dogmatic marxism identifies power with property, while the bourgeois point of view attempts to derive ownership from power. Marx's analysis of bureaucracy, on the other hand, is an excellent demonstration of the dialectical relationship between ownership and power. Property ownership, as a historically developed and defined and substantive system of the relations of production, creates different types of power, but these have no automatic or personal relationship to the enforcement of the property rights of individuals. Institutions of state administration, as well as economic, military, political and other institutions, develop historically in a wide variety of social and economic forms, within which power relationships not directly connected to the private property of individuals take on the appearance of real power.

However, before the different types of bureaucracy in a country can possess real power and not merely execute the will of the property owner or the property-owning class, the right historical conditions must exist. This occurred in mid-nineteenth century Prussia, where bureaucratic possession of power developed and was maintained as a result of insufficiently developed conditions of bourgeois society in that country: the old feudal relationships had already lost their ascendancy, but new relationships had not yet ripened sufficiently to take their place. The result was a peculiar situation in which the princely states were still fighting kingdoms, bureaucratic officialdom was at war with the nobility, the bourgeoisie was struggling against all of them, while the proletariat had already entered the lists against the bourgeoisie.

Thereafter, the Prussian state bureaucracy, on which Marx's analysis had largely been based, no longer played an active role. Moreover, the social function of the state administration in Germany, where backward social conditions prevailed, differed from that played by the bureaucracy during the disintegration of feudalism and the beginning of the centralisation of state power. At

14

that time, through its opposition to the traditional forms of governing, it had unambiguously served the objectives of progress and its primary function had been to help establish commodity relations on a firm footing and to assist in the related task of integrating the nation-state.

Having fulfilled the historical functions for which it came into being, the bureaucracy nonetheless—or perhaps because of this—continued to strive to retain its power. One of the principal ways in which it did this was through the monopolisation and mystification of the bureaucratic profession—a twin process which has inevitably followed the emergence of a bureaucracy and bureaucratic relationships down to the present day. This, in turn, has repeatedly produced a counter-reaction and efforts on the part of various classes and strata in society to break down the monopoly of the administrative function and to obtain a clear and comprehensive picture of the professional problems of administration.

Thus it is clear why Marx, as editor of the *Neue Rheinische Zeitung*, repeatedly emphasised the importance of breaking down the professional monopoly of étatist bureaucracy as well as the importance of demystifying it.

The later periods in Marx's life, when he turned to the investigation of developed bourgeois societies, based on the experience of England and France, which was to result in the brilliant analyses of *Capital*, were to produce no more detailed discussions on bureaucracy or state administration. This did not mean he repudiated his earlier conclusions on the subject—rather, he felt that the real momentum of developed capitalism originated in the struggle between capitalist and worker, in the face of which bureaucracy had no choice but to act formally and negatively: "Where bourgeois life and activity begin, [the] power [of the state bureaucracy] ends." In *The Eighteenth Brumaire of Louis Bonaparte*, he commented on the bureaucracy as it had developed under classical capitalism: "This executive power with its vast bureaucratic and military organisation, far-reaching and artificial state machinery, of officials amounting to half a million members, in addition to armed forces of equal number, is a terrific parasitical body which entangles the body of French society like a net and obstructs its power."

The present century has witnessed the emergence of a historically new socio-economic formation, the socialist system, but the problem of bureaucracy has by no means disappeared with it, although it manifests itself in fundamentally different ways. We can still make use of Marx's brilliant analysis of the bureaucracy of his era in order to understand the substantive relations inherent in this new situation; and without applying his statements in an unhistorical way, we can adapt his methods to an analysis of the present situation. On this basis, we shall be able to determine the essential nature of bureaucracy in the socialist society whose purpose is to serve the interests of socialist development.

II: Historical Antecedents of the Fight against Bureaucracy

The great revolutionaries and rebels of class societies were in full agreement about one thing, almost without exception. In the new society which would emerge as the result of social progress, there would be no need for society to be run and the state to be administered by a leadership separate from those directly engaged in production, a leadership possessing particular interests and maintaining a bureaucratic relation to the rest of the people. In all European revolutionary movements, from the plebeian democrat Thomas Münzer onwards, the idea that, in the new society, all power would be transferred to the people, has remained alive.

There have been many different ideas about how to rehumanise the power which has been alienated. Münzer dreamed of an alliance of democratic communities, in which the highest executive power would be the collectivity of the citizens. Rousseau wanted the "old, natural" conditions back, the democratic era of Greek and Roman society where the direct power of the people was a reality. "We have to find that form of community", he wrote, "which defends with its collective power the persons and property of all its members and in which everybody, even when united with others, obeys only himself and remains as free as before."[4]

The idea that the state could be administered and society run without bureaucratic relations, a society which is socialised and rehumanised in the fullest sense of the word, has always been a revolutionary one, rooted in the criticism of existing conditions. It has become a source of inspiration for revolutionary movements serving social progress. The vision of it is a moving experience, even when the utopia has proved to be unreachable and history has showed it to be an illusion. The utopian character of these ideas became historically obvious only when the movements inspired by them began to gain victories in the various social struggles and when the realisation of the vision became a realistic political goal.

The French revolution is a typical, concentrated form of this confrontation between ideas and actual social possibilities. In a period of about half a decade, France went through all the processes which took several centuries in Britain and several decades (rather belatedly) in Germany.

In order to stay in power, the Jacobin dictatorship gradually had to discard the broad application of democratic rights by means of which it had triumphed. A grotesque historical situation arose in which representatives of the reaction were able to speak out as champions of the demand to extend democracy. However, during the period of these struggles, the special interest of the administration as a "separate" power managing society had not yet appeared in a fully developed form, though it existed in embryo. At this stage of development the social apparatus for administrative functions had not emerged as a bearer of the actual relations of power, and therefore the fight against it necessarily continued to be of secondary importance. The idea of social administration, and the need for it, could only be formulated definitely in the advanced bourgeois societies, where the bureaucracy took forms and functions which were different from those it took during the struggle against feudalism.

After the Jacobin dictatorship had fallen, a new bureaucratic apparatus emerged in France with incredible speed, already fulfilling its social administrative functions in the interest of the new ruling class, the capitalists. Just fifty years later, Marx stated in *The Eighteenth Brumaire of Louis Bonaparte* that "the executive power commands an army of more than half a million officials . . . and keeps in absolute dependence a mighty mass of people all the time. . . . The state entangles, controls, supervises and keeps watch over the bourgeois society, from the broadest manifestation of its existence to its smallest stirrings, from its most general forms of life to the private lives of individuals."[5]

In 1871 the people of Paris revolted not only against capitalist rule but also against the bureaucratic power which protected it. They tried to put into practice their ideas about the administration of society without bureaucratic relations. It is no accident that it was Blanqui, the most important theoretician of the Paris Commune, who first formulated a programme for the attack on bureaucracy (in his *Critique Sociale*). He demanded that the upper and middle strata of officials should be subject to direct election and recall, while the lower strata should hold their jobs only temporarily. In spite of this, even for Blanqui, it was a secondary question, the primary one being the seizure of power: political power was a question of much greater importance to him than what sort of new order to establish in the society of the future. (This is a clear indication of his "revolutionism", for which Marx held him in such esteem.) In the second half of the last century the debate about representative and direct democracy turned on the question of how to realise the final goal of power, not on how democratic institutions could exert control over administration and management, which brought with them bureaucratic relations and were penetrating into more and more spheres of social life.

In this century bureaucracy has become increasingly powerful. It has reduced the representative institutions of the Western capitalist countries (whose task was originally to protect the bourgeoisie's interests) to a formality, either openly as in fascism or covertly as in the bourgeois democracies, and it has even deprived them of their functions as defenders of the ruling class.

Administration, as the bearer of bureaucratic relations, has also gained ground in the economy; the traditional management of factories by owner-directors has been replaced by special apparatuses which were at first divided along hierarchical lines and later along functional ones too. This ensured that affairs were run better (according to Max Weber, more quickly, more efficiently and with more skill); but at the same time, the more power that management acquired in practical matters, the more it found itself opposed to the shareholders and their representatives (supervisory bodies, etc.).

The development of bureaucratism has entered a new phase, with the mass media (large-circulation newspapers, periodicals, best-sellers, radio, films and television) regarding it as their special task to "influence" and manipulate public opinion. Hierarchic apparatuses have mushroomed into existence in order to carry out this task. They are in reality a new form of power, the power over people's souls.

Bureaucratic relations in the socialist revolution

While dogmatic marxists were unwilling to take notice of these new phenomena which had necessarily occurred in the course of capitalist development, the reformist marxists created reformist policies based precisely on these developments. Meanwhile the revolutionary movement which had adopted marxist ideology scored a victory of historic importance in a country where not only Western-type bureaucracy but also the industrial bourgeoisie itself was underdeveloped.

This victory gave a whole new meaning and importance to the question of bureaucracy. In the biggest and one of the most backward countries of the world, the October revolution removed the ruling classes and their private property and, with them, the industrial bourgeoisie, before the latter could bring its fight against feudal privileges to a successful conclusion and even before it had a chance to industrialise the country. These factors proved to be of overwhelming importance in later developments, but during the revolutionary struggles of the time they were of secondary importance in comparison with the primary objective, which was to establish workers' and peasants' power.

True to their historical traditions, marxism-leninism and the revolutionary movement which found its inspiration there were guided by the aim of destroying not only private property and the classes based on it but also the state apparatus which till then had carried out the work of class oppression. What also had to be prevented was any governing or administrative apparatus arising which might become the possessor of particular interests and aims separate from society, from the direct producers themselves. This idea appears quite explicitly in Lenin's writings from before the proletarian revolution: "Under socialism much of 'primitive' democracy will inevitably be revived, since, for the first time in the history of civilised society, the *mass* of the population will rise to taking an *independent* part, not only in voting and elections, *but also in the everyday administration of the state.* Under socialism *all* will govern in turn and will soon become accustomed to no one governing."[6]

But practical experience after the socialist revolution did not enable this evidently ideal situation to be realised. The need for a stable and disciplined state apparatus against foreign invasion existed, but the literature on this period gives a very one-sided emphasis to this factor. The other reason why the ideal was not realised was that a skilled government body was needed to rehabilitate and develop the economy and many other branches of social life.

This historical necessity led inevitably, however, to the reappearance of bureaucratic relations. That is to say, the conditions were created for a situation in which the government and administrative apparatus developed its own interests and aims, which are not always identical with the interests and aims of the society as a whole.

It can easily be proved that, at a time when the revolutionary movement still had illusions about the future, Lenin had already perceived the danger of such bureaucratic relations existing and predominating. It was still being supposed that direct people's government would become a general reality within a relatively short space of time; and it was inevitable that the maintenance of these illusions would be linked tightly to the question of defending workers' and peasants' power. But especially after the introduction of NEP, Lenin was considerably preoccupied with the idea that the Soviet Union would need an educated and competent administration. This was the period when he spoke out strongly for the necessity of adopting the Taylor system. He fully knew that the original function of taylorism is to make people sweat. At the same time, however, he knew that the Soviet economy could not be raised to a high level without the skills of its leadership being improved; all the experience of the capitalist world had to be made use of. An educated and effective administration, separated from society, had to come into being. Lenin knew that the only thing that could prevent it from becoming the bearer of bureaucratic relations was to set up institutions, before it happened, which would bring about social control over the administration, thereby providing a permanent and effective force which would prevent the bureaucratic relations from rigidifying and becoming autocratic.

In this sense, the problem of bureaucratic relations had already been formulated in the first years of Soviet power, and was becoming an increasingly controversial issue in Soviet society. "The development of the spontaneous activity of the masses will become possible only if we eradicate from the face of the earth those bureaucratic blemishes known as 'glavki' and 'centres'." This is a sentence from a report written and sent to Lenin by Sokolov, who was the secretary of an organisation controlling the evacuation from Poland. He was a young man who had made "two or three futile attempts" to fight against bureaucracy. The essence of Lenin's reply, which has often been quoted for various different purposes, was that in a peasant country, bureaucracy "cannot be chased away" or "wiped off the earth"[7]: it can only be decreased by slow, steady work. In his debates with Trotsky and Bukharin in 1920 Lenin went further, saying that the Soviet state was not a workers' state but "a workers' state with bureaucratic excesses", from which he drew the conclusion that the trade unions would have to protect themselves against their own state and, by relying on the workers, to defend the workers' state against foreign intervention.

The social basis of bureaucratic relations in socialism

The experiences of the socialist society which have accumulated

21

over the decades since then show that Lenin's concern was not unfounded. In the interpretation of marxist sociology, the development of bureaucratic social relations is a necessity, but they play a quite different part from that which they played in previous eras. Two questions need to be answered if we are to analyse the problem correctly. In an already established socialist society, is there any need for an apparatus separate from those directly engaged in production and in the service sector, fulfilling the functions of government and administration which stem from the social division of labour? And if so, can it be considered necessary that the apparatus fulfilling this function should have its own interests and aims and that it should be the bearer of bureaucratic relations? There is ample enough historical experience to answer both questions, which means that there is every reason to support the demand for a confrontation between theory and this experience in justifying whatever standpoint one takes.

The emergence of bureaucratic relations in socialism is determined by the fact that the newly established form of socialist ownership does not give the lawful proprietors (whether the state, the people or a co-operative) any possibility of exercising their property rights directly. This is the case regardless of the level of development, and over the whole of society (including the co-operative peasants). These rights are transferred, even if it is in their own interests, to a professionally skilled group which exercises the administration of society. At the same time the emergence of state ownership in the socialist countries allows an incomparably higher degree of integration than before, even in countries where the level of productive forces is less developed; this fact in itself increases the importance of the administrative and management functions of the society.

Although the creation of social (state and co-operative) property brought about a fundamentally new situation in productive relations, it did not by itself prevent the emergence or existence of an administration separated from society; in fact it made it even more necessary. At the present stage of development of the socialist countries, administration and management can only be carried out by some kind of specially "exempt" apparatus; direct social administration, as a basic form of government, can only be carried out in a relatively restricted area of social life. Therefore, no matter how attractive the attempt at direct social self-government is, in the present condition of society illusions necessarily dominate in this respect. In practice, what is possible is merely a more or less effective control over the administration: this is nevertheless in itself a very important step towards the humanisation of administration and management.

In almost every field of social life in the socialist countries, there is a special, hierarchised and increasingly standardised form of administration, and this is especially noticeable in the apparatus of local councils and the agricultural co-operatives. It is in precisely these areas that the maintenance of direct social administration and management is still believed to be possible, through the rotation of posts. But even here, this has not been borne out by experience. There is actually an increasing demand for the chairmen of councils and co-operatives to be qualified people. It is an achievement to have enough people to meet these requirements, and society cannot afford the luxury of replacing them regularly with manual workers or paying them the same rates as skilled workers. Nowadays a large majority of the people newly appointed to these posts have previously worked in similar areas or have climbed the hierarchical ladder of the administration.

Contrary to general belief, it does not always have to be the case that bureaucracy breeds bad work or uneconomical results. A special, hierarchised and standardised administration which is necessarily separated from working people can work very efficiently in socialism, even if society's control over it is purely formal. And it often tends to be more efficient if bureaucracy is freed from the "fetters" of social control. On the other hand, the socialist character of property demands that management itself should be socialised and that the bureaucratic relations should therefore be gradually removed, even if the one-sided bureaucratic solution of administrative problems seems more efficient. In this respect too, then, a real contradiction between "optimisation" and "humanisation" appears.

If we say that a form of management involving bureaucratic relations necessarily arises in socialism, that does not mean that we are denying the existence of the extremely important distinction between the bureaucratic relations of capitalism and those of socialism, and between the forms of administration which bear these relations. The management and administration of society in socialism and the bureaucratic relations involved have very specific features, which go beyond the original starting point of the administrative system in the socialist states. This starting point was the dictatorship of the proletariat, which crushed the bourgeois system of administration and virtually liquidated (though not in the physical sense of the word) the old bureaucracy, while workers, peasants and revolutionary intellectuals built up a new, socialist

23

system of government, taking over the functions of management and administration in the name of the society of working people. Although this beginning is very important for the society, it does not exclude the possibility of further changes in various alternative directions, as history has shown us.

Bureaucratic relations in administration arise inevitably, because the construction of an administrative apparatus that is separated from the direct producers is an objective necessity at this stage of development: but the character of these bureaucratic relations, their place and their role in social relations generally, is fundamentally different from the character of bureaucracy in class societies, on account of the essential characteristics of the system and the existing property relations. The enemies of socialism only look at these differences in the light of the fact that in the socialist countries there is increased integration as a result of centralisation, with more power concentrated in the administrative apparatus. They do not look at the extremely strong social forces which pressurise the administration bearing these bureaucratic relations into sharing its power, into socialising its management activities and finally, as the result of a long historical development, eliminating itself as a bureaucracy.

The existing level of the division of labour and of property relations lead one to deduce not only that the continuation of bureaucratic relations is necessary, but also that the specific features of this social relation are characteristic of socialism alone. The proprietor in whose name the representatives of administration and management proceed is no longer the head of a patriarchal state, no longer the king as the "chief nobleman" of feudal society, and no longer the capitalist companies or the capitalist class, but the whole (national) society or a certain social group within it (e.g., a co-operative), whose members are equal to each other in terms of the property relations.

One of the basic criteria for the existence of bureaucratic relations in the socialist system of administration is the separation between the administration and the working people as proprietors. This separation does not necessarily imply a closed process from the subjective point of view, a conscious confrontation with the working people. The bureaucracy in capitalist society, to use a crude analogy, does not stand in definitive opposition to the capitalist proprietors and their representative organs either. In a socialist society it is absolutely obvious that the administrative apparatus must reach all its decisions in the interest of society. To a large extent this is not unjustified, for the interest of society as interpreted by this apparatus is in fact an important motive of its activities. Even when it follows particular interests, the administrative apparatus always acts in the name of the common interest, and the reasons for the contradiction between goals of this kind and its real goals are more complicated than in the case of state and management bureaucracy in the capitalist countries.

The administrative organs of socialist society act on the authority of the whole society as proprietor, and in fact play an incomparably more positive role than the bureaucracies of previous eras. Precisely for this reason, it is more difficult to dig out from behind the real general interest of the society those particular interests which are aimed at maintaining or even strengthening the bureaucratic relations. The situation is complicated by the administration's attempts at increased efficiency, as a result of which (as I point out elsewhere) the particular interest often appears in a special form and, under certain historical conditions, is capable of becoming general.

Negative consequences of the bureaucratic relation

Everyday thinking takes this extraordinarily complicated and contradictory movement and registers only those phenomena which emerge as unambiguously negative in everyday life, with the result that a stereotyped bureaucrat emerges. But only a deeper analysis of bureaucratic relations can give an authentic account of the phenomena which everyday thinking, in a one-sided and pejorative concept, regards as the typical features of bureaucratic procedure.

The most striking feature, the mechanical treatment of citizens as "clients", basically reflects the bureaucratic "dependency" relation. The "client" is conceived as some kind of strange outsider, or even some downright malevolent person, over whom the administration, as the representative of the whole society, holds power. In most cases, of course, this mystified social interest represents a much greater power for the individual official than it did for a king ruling by divine right or any capitalist company. And to make the situation more grotesque and complicated, this tendency to make a derived power absolute often penetrates much more deeply into the lower ranks of the hierarchy than into the upper ones. The lower ranks are inclined to take out on the client their lack of a substantial deciding voice in the administrative system.

Another well-known feature of bureaucracy is procrastination in handling business, the fear of making decisions, the bureaucratic delays. This can easily be deduced from the special conditions temporarily prevailing within the hierarchy. It is usually strong at times when the rules of procedure have not been established and, as a result, the required "pattern" of action undergoes rapid changes. This causes people to be more vulnerable if their decisions are "erroneous" for some unforeseen reason (e.g., a change in the criteria for making estimates) than if they do not make decisions or can cover themselves with dozens of signatures. The objective circumstances can often make the outcome of decisions unclear (this is often demonstrated in matters concerning economic management).

But neither the snubbing of "clients" nor the red tape can be regarded as an inevitable feature of the essential relations of bureaucracy. The situation is not inconceivable where it might be the official's highest duty to "deal with" or "manipulate" the customer with the utmost scientific method—but bureaucracy would still be the basic relation between society and the administration, and could not be said to be outdated: it would in fact be appearing in its most explicit form. Similarly, the basic relations within the administration would not be changed (though its efficiency might increase considerably) if the higher ranks of the hierarchy expected—and obtained, in general practice—promptness and responsible decision-making of an ideal Weberian type.

One of the most serious consequences of the bureaucratisation of society is the exaggerated tendency to conform (which is itself a necessary occurrence). Marx gave a brilliant analysis of the ways in which a bureaucrat tries to accommodate himself to the supposed or real norms which he unreservedly accepts, even to the extent of suppressing his own individuality completely. In modern capitalism this feature has broken out of the relatively narrow limits of the state bureaucracy; conformism in the true sense of the word has become a general phenomenon. This state of affairs can in no way be said to have become outdated in socialism either.

On the basis of all this, we can say that the administrative and management apparatus of the socialist state essentially derives from the character of property relations, and that it is the bearer of attempts to establish both bureaucratic and humanised relations. This means that administration presents itself both as bureaucracy and as non-bureaucracy. Unless this essential contradiction is disclosed, virtually nothing can be understood about the history of the socialist countries' development, and those who make one or the other side of this contradiction absolute will draw inevitably false conclusions.

How to overcome the present conditions: possibilities and difficulties

From what I have said above, it directly follows that if we take into account the functions fulfilled by the administration as the bearer of bureaucratic relations, we cannot evaluate the latter simply as a negative phenomenon which must be classified as "bad" as opposed to some other category of "good". We must see it as a social formation which arises necessarily and which can be overcome by quite specific social conditions, not simply by rational thinking or good will.

At the present stage of development of the productive forces and of the social division of labour, two seemingly contradictory social necessities present themselves. On the one hand, the rights, responsibilities and competence, and consequently the efficiency, of administration must be extended, even if this results in the strengthening of bureaucratic relations or in their temporary rigidification. On the other hand, the administration and its various instances must be made dependent on society, i.e., it must be gradually humanised so as to bring about the decay of the bureaucratic relations. These historically simultaneous tasks may lead, under certain social conditions, to conflict. It often occurs that, on the grounds of political expediency (which may or may not be well-founded), one criterion can only be realised at the expense of the other. But even then the confrontation between them leads, in the last analysis, to a false set of alternatives. On no occasion has historical experience ever demonstrated that one must necessarily choose between the two, even in the short term. The social interest usually demands that both requirements be taken into account simultaneously. This may seem to contradict what I have said elsewhere about putting the primary emphasis on the problem of humanisation and of restricting the sphere of the bureaucratic relations. But I am aware that this is just one way of approaching the question, not the only way, and that the solution of this question is inseparable from the need to speed up the development of the productive forces and to meet the requirements of optimisation.

There is a campaign currently in full swing in the socialist countries against bureaucracy; there are articles, cartoons and jokes all aimed at exposing bureaucratic practices. It is due in no small way to this campaign that everyday thinking has created a popular image of the bureaucrat as the official who always shelves documents, is afraid of responsibility, kowtows to his superiors and is rude and overbearing to his subordinates. Very few people however, even among the consistent opponents of bureaucracy, take into account the fact that these features are simply the by-product of an administration which is separate from the ultimate guarantor of power, i.e., society: a society in which a hierarchic relationship of subordinates and superiors has necessarily formed, with its positive and negative sides, either because there is no social control at the various levels or else because this control is purely formal. As a result, the "sense of responsibility" exists only in respect of carrying out the orders of the higher organs. If this is the case, then the "client"—he might be an employee in the same office or simply someone who is within the official's jurisdiction—is necessarily just someone opposed to the official, and at best he is merely shown "mercy". This kind of administration which is separated from its proprietors—the working people —creates all the negative phenomena which we have referred to. For the same reason, bureaucratic phenomena can only be surmounted by means of the overall development of social relations and institutions, through a relatively long process. The scope for the influence of education is at least, in terms of society as a whole, too narrow.

Under capitalist property relations the fight against bureaucracy is futile, since the development of productive forces goes hand in hand with a broader and more intensive domination of bureaucratic relations in almost every sphere of social life. The precondition for the elimination of this trend is to abolish private ownership of the means of production, of the basic social relationship which gives authority to certain people (the owners) or their representatives (the bureaucrats) to rule over other people. All respect and attention is due to those thinkers, sociologists and writers who have rebelled against bureaucracy, this modern form of inhumanity, but if they do not speak up for the abolition of private ownership at the same time, they will inevitably remain stuck in the realm of petty bourgeois utopias or abstract moralising.

However, abolition of private ownership of the means of production (or at least its position as the main form of property) is only the first step. It is only a starting point for the overall humanisation of social relations. Whoever claims that the abolition of private ownership has automatically done away with the alienated social relations sooner or later turns into a one-sided and conservative defender of the bureaucratic relations. Both the revisionists and the anarchists (the spiritual forefathers of contemporary "leftist" revolutionaries) flatly reject, though from different standpoints, the very question of whether it is possible to eradicate bureaucracy in the socialist society. Bernstein "felt all right" in the presence of bureaucratic relations, and considered it pointless to discuss fighting against them, while the anarchists (e.g. Sorel) held that any kind of organisation would produce bureaucracy, and since they regarded it as one of the greatest evils possible they proclaimed war on any kind of organisation or institution.

In capitalism, bureaucracy has bred reform and revisionism in the working-class movement; in socialism, it has strengthened dogmatism by replacing the promotion of socialist development with the defence of the existing forms. The fact that social administration and management generate bureaucratic relations is a *historical* phenomenon: they have been brought about inevitably by the development of society, i.e. by the development of property relations at a given stage in the division of labour and economic integration. Therefore, a stage of development also has to come (and its outlines can already be seen in the socialist countries) when there will be no need for an administration separate from society, because the objective and subjective conditions will be ripe for the consistent realisation of social self-administration. Nevertheless, although the creation of socialist property relations was a big step in this direction, we have not yet reached this stage.

In Marx's words, "Bureaucracy can only be abolished if the general interest becomes in reality (and not only in thought, in abstraction, as Hegel claims) a special interest, which is only possible if the special interest becomes, in reality, the general interest."[8] In the European socialist societies, the division of labour determined by the present level of the productive forces and income differentials do not yet make it possible to meet this requirement. Particular interests still arise within the administration more or less as a matter of course. This prevents the general interest of society from always becoming a "special" interest of the administration; and very often it also prevents the particular interest from appearing in a "special" form through which it might in time become general.

This does not mean, however, that we lack the forces with which to curb this tendency and keep it within certain limits. The weakening of the bureaucratic character of administration, as an objective and necessary social tendency in the course of a long historical period, will take place in various ways, and it will come about in the course of the struggle between conflicting social forces. In this struggle, the greatest influence is that which is exerted by the communist workers' parties. In the socialist societies, these organisations group together the most progressive people who base themselves on marxist theory; they are not only the vanguard of economic development in the narrow sense, but also of social progress in the widest sense, and of the many-sided growth of the essential forces of man.

It is understandable that bureaucratic relations are easier to overcome in the party organisations, the youth movement and the trade unions, i.e. (broadly speaking) in the social organisations in general. This does not, of course, mean that it would be impossible for bureaucracy to spring up in the administration of these organisations. It goes without saying that the circumstances which breed bureaucratic relations in socialism have their influence in these organisations too. But the weakening of bureaucratic administration becomes a social necessity much more directly here, and its preconditions ripen much sooner here than in the sphere of management. In the latter, the accumulation of bureaucratic relations does not necessarily decrease efficiency, but in the social organisations it undoubtedly produces the kind of distortion in their activities that prevents them from fulfilling their basic tasks. Much depends in this respect on whether these organisations can discern and articulate the necessity in time, and on whether they can prevent the almost "spontaneous" emergence of bureaucracy in the party and the mass organisation. Since the Twentieth Congress of the CPSU many changes have taken place to counter this tendency in most of the European socialist countries (and not least in Hungary), especially in the development of social institutions and the democratisation of public life.

It is increasingly being recognised that however important the explanation or exposure of bureaucratic errors might be, the results are only temporary. In order to prevent the rapid growth of bureaucratic tendencies there is a need first of all for a continuous development of the social institutions, for a modernisation of the administration (though, understandably, the main aim of the "reform" proposals is to increase efficiency, to "optimise"). In my opinion the main means of bringing about the decay of bureaucratic relations are gradually coming to the fore, and they are as follows:

(1) The institutional pressure on the administration and management to share their power. The first requirement for this is the efficient functioning of the present forms of control (supervision

by the party, trade union and works committees, etc.), and the exposure and elimination of disturbing factors in cases where this functioning has become purely formal.

The idea of the democratisation of administration and the development of the self-administration of the society is always an attack on hierarchic control and therefore on bureaucratic relations, although it does not mean the immediate socialisation of administration. If it becomes reality, it disrupts the internal hierarchic relations, brings about social control from outside at various levels, and is thus directed against the essence of bureaucracy, the consolidation of bureaucratic relations.

Certain sections of the administration, however, continually attempt to oppose these aims (which reflects not only their subjective shortcomings but also the essence of the bureaucratic relations), and to render these organs of social control purely formal in some way or other. In order to achieve this aim they cite both practical arguments (the fetish of expertise) and ideological ones too (the defence of the principle of "adhering to the plan", centralism, etc.).

The outlines of the new institutional forms of control, which at this stage of development seem to promise more efficiency than the generally accepted solutions, can only be elaborated on the basis of an overall analysis of the existing situation. Unless this kind of analysis is made, it is inconceivable that conscious progress, really corresponding to the aims of socialist development, can be achieved. But progress on the basis of scientific analysis is also hampered by the fact that this analysis is influenced by viewpoints reflecting the already established bureaucratic relations. It therefore often avoids exposing the most substantial bureaucratic interconnections, and fails to work out the correct conclusions. For example, the recently established National Technological Development Board* will be able to work out forecasts of technological development which will be valuable for society if the experts doing this job can get rid of the narrow bureaucratic mentality. For the same reason, sociological research (particularly in law, social science and economics) which is partisan in the marxist sense of the term might be of great importance when it is freed from the rule of bureaucratic relations.

(2) One of the important means of overcoming bureaucratic relations is to secure a healthy mobility in every sphere of the administration. The marxist classics attribute great importance to

---

* This is the Hungarian equivalent of a Ministry of Technology.

the possibility of replacing officials. The Yugoslav experiment is well-known. It tries to put into practice a "rotation" principle by which (to simplify it somewhat) those who have occupied a post for four years must occupy a different one for the next four. Many people argue against this principle, claiming that the efficiency of the administration requires greater stability of personnel. This argument is not without foundation (we can see once again how the criteria of "optimisation" and "humanisation" conflict). But it can only be accepted as true for a narrow stratum of the administration: for the most part, administration involves the sort of functions where a planned rotation of official personnel is expedient not only for the sake of opposing bureaucratic tendencies but also for the sake of greater efficiency.

(3) The greatest obstacle to the rapid growth and ossification of bureaucratic relations is the development of democratism in public life; that is to say, the creation of the kind of atmosphere in society which will prevent expert knowledge from having a monopoly in any sphere of administration and will make the unlimited rule of hierarchic conditions impossible. Of course, attempts to develop democratism in public life clash with the contradiction that we have already discussed many times over: it often seems to take the form of incompetent interventions which hamper the administration's efficiency. And we can find a lot of truth in this if we look at certain cases. But this does not alter the fact that efforts to extend the democratisation of public life are necessary and basically progressive.

All three possibilities discussed here can become reality only if the party, as the most advanced organisation of the progressive forces of society, adopts them as aims. From this viewpoint, the developments which took place in the Hungarian Socialist Workers' Party in the years after 1956 can and should be regarded in a positive light; it was a period when the problem of overcoming bureaucratic relations was tackled, which shifted the whole problem from the realm of slogans to the realm of realities.

The social conditions under which the bureaucratic relations of management become outdated, as the result of long historical development and struggle, will not be a simple historical renewal of the direct ("primitive", in Lenin's words) democracy of the clan system, but the rehumanisation of all social relations and functions (including administration and management), by means of the development of the essential human forces to an incomparably higher stage of social progress.

The marxist analysis of bureaucratic relations in socialism, and the attempts to overcome their existence in the administrative system of the socialist societies, are necessary for one other very important reason. This is that new comrades and supporters of marxism must be found on a larger scale, especially among the working class of the developed capitalist countries, and also among those who criticise the bureaucratic relations of modern capitalist society from a petty bourgeois, romantic standpoint. This is an important precondition for bringing home the idea of socialism to these social strata in the highly developed capitalist countries. Their opinion is of great importance, for among them there are people who seem to lose faith in socialism: not simply because of the bureaucratic relations which exist in it, but because of the apologetics which are made for these relations and which are in fact inconsistent with marxism, however widespread they may be.

III: Economic Management and Social Control

In my article "Optimisation and Humanisation"[9] I tried to argue that demands for both an increase in the efficiency of management and a many-sided rehumanisation of social relations appear simultaneously in the socialist society out of historical necessity—that is, not as the result of some subjective thought process, but from objective causes. Although these demands can ultimately be seen to complement and depend upon each other, conflict between them is common and it often appears as if one can only be realised at the expense of the other.

The source of this opposition lies in the fact that in the socialist countries, which are still stratified societies—in which separate and different interest groups continue to exist—the various social groups do not embody these demands to an equal degree. Workers employed in the administrative or managerial apparatus, for example, are—simply as a result of their functions—concerned first and foremost with how they can raise the efficiency of their activity. On the other hand that section of the intelligentsia which works outside of such institutions (writers, journalists, doctors, social science researchers, etc.)—again simply because of the nature of its tasks—expresses an interest first of all in the humanisation of social relations.

The first criterion—the raising of efficiency—demands a special administrative apparatus, one which is both scientifically organised and hierarchically structured, which has both highly qualified personnel and a regulated mode of operation. This, however, inevitably leads to the creation of social forces which set themselves in opposition to the fulfilment of the second criterion, i.e. in opposition to the incorporation of the direct producers in decision-making processes (more precisely, the self-management of society) and to the various forms of social control (parliament, local councils, the party, etc.).

It is perhaps precisely in this pair of concepts—in the conflicting demands of "sophisticated" administration and management, and "social control" over the apparatus which carries out these functions—that the contradictions between the criteria of optimisation and humanisation find their most important expression in socialist society. There can be little doubt that the implementation of this dual requirement is one of the most pressing problems in the development of socialism today—a period which, by all indications, the future history of the European socialist countries will describe as the period of economic reform. Of course we cannot exclude the possibility that one or other of the demands may temporarily gain precedence.

In order to disentangle this complex set of questions we must first make a brief if schematic survey, from this point of view, of half a century of development in the Soviet Union, as well as two decades of development in the European socialist countries. This is a long period of time if we compare it to a man's present life expectation, or a short one if we compare it to the history of mankind, but either way it seems to be long enough for the most important characteristics of the development of this socio-economic formation to become identifiable. The socialist countries of Europe have now reached that stage which is important in the development of any society and which capitalism had reached in Marx's day, when the critical analysis of its own relations becomes possible.

In the history of the Soviet state after the old bourgeois state power had been destroyed, the first demand to arise was the need for an efficient and centralised administration (in the given situation, the two were identical). For what were very sound reasons, in 1920 Lenin came out against the principle of a producers' democracy. The strengthening of one-man management was at that time a matter of life or death for the survival of the Soviet state. The party had to choose this course even at the price of establishing bureaucratic relations. All the same, there could be no greater error, and nothing more contradictory to Lenin's way of thinking, than for us to consider this point of view as a law valid for the whole period of socialism (though, incidentally, we can meet with many attempts to do just this).

In the years immediately following the proletarian revolution the demand for humanisation could not even present itself, if only because it was, after all, assumed that this had already been realised in the socialist state. From the beginning of the twenties, Lenin already sensed the groundlessness of this assumption, but he did not have the time to give complete and concrete expression to his doubts. His ideas took shape primarily in the course of debates about particular institutions, such as the "trade union debate" and the problem of developing the organisational forms of the worker-peasant inspectorate.

The special apparatus for dealing with the tasks of economic

35

management in the Soviet Union took a strongly centralised form, one which in the underdeveloped conditions of tsarist Russia we could justifiably consider a historical necessity. Centralisation played a progressive role here too, as it has on more than one occasion in history. Without wanting to make any sort of fanciful analogy, I mention the fact that Marx recognised the centralism of the absolute monarchy as a "civilising activity".

Whatever the objective historical conditions that caused it, the development of the strongly centralised form of administration is nevertheless of secondary importance. The most basic need, which is of equal importance in all socialist countries, is the construction of an administrative and managerial apparatus which is hierarchically structured and specialised according to the division of labour. To express this in a different way: in the most important aspects of managing society it was not possible to handle the administrative and managerial functions on a socialised basis. Specially trained experts were necessary for this, men who were totally devoted to their jobs and who, because they occupied a particular place in the social division of labour, had their own particular interests and aims.

It is another question whether in this period it was possible to conceive of the incorporation of the workers into administrative and managerial functions as historically necessary or, if it was possible, what form this could have taken. The establishment of socialist property relations, i.e. the abolition of private ownership of the major means of production, irrespective of whether they become state or co-operative property, in itself requires the socialisation of all forms of power. This includes the power that is created by the function of managing economic activity. If their socialisation is not possible, then at least their subjection to social supervision is required. Many factors hinder the realisation of this —not least the very opposition between the special apparatus performing administrative and managerial functions and the various forms of social management and supervision. On top of this, the social conditions necessary for the full realisation of these demands cannot be considered ripe enough in every respect (I am thinking of the state of development of relations of commitment and consciousness). All these causes contributed to the fact that in most of the socialist countries of Europe, where administration and management developed in a hierarchically structured and centralised form, social supervision was able to play only a very limited role; its main (indeed almost its only) form was the political supervision carried out by the various organs of the communist workers' parties,

36

beside which even trade union activity became of secondary importance.

Because the apparatus of economic management, with its special, skilled knowledge and its own interests, strives for autonomy, and indeed in some cases for a position of monopoly, it comes into opposition with the working of the trade unions and with party supervision, which both want to establish social control. As yet we have few methodological studies from which we can learn how far we can generalise from individual experiences. Nevertheless, it seems valid to conclude that the more the characteristics of the administration (specialisation, standardisation, hierarchisation, etc.) come to prevail in any system of economic management, then the more the various forms of social control will turn into purely formal ones. This would seem to be the case as regards both party supervision and trade union activity. Indeed, there are inevitably attempts to get these organs to recognise the achievements of the administration's activity without any reservations whatever. Of course this does not mean that these types of economic institution cannot work with professional efficiency. Indeed, on more than one occasion it has been precisely those organs which registered appreciable success in fulfilling their own functions that have manifested the greatest opposition to social supervision and control.

It is worth noting here that, in contrast to accepted beliefs in Hungary about bureaucracy, Max Weber argued that a bureaucratically organised administration has three advantages over the traditional one, namely that it is characterised by speed, expertise and efficiency. Though we cannot accept these properties as always characteristic of bureaucratic administrative relations, neither should we believe that slowness, amateurishness and inefficiency are necessarily the attributes of any administration that has been separated from society by the division of labour.

The problems of today would remain incomprehensible if we could not construct a realistic picture of the causes and developmental characteristics of the appearance of this phenomenon—that is, the growth in power and significance of administration and management. One of the greatest weaknesses of everyday thinking is that it can only move between false alternatives: in this instance, the false choice between historical necessity and subjective (and thus chance) errors. History is the end result of the struggles of social forces representing the interests of different groups, and it is in this sense that people really do "make their own history".

In this battle, objective necessity gives a hand to one side or the other; but in the majority of cases it does not unambiguously decide the outcome of the struggle. The outcome of history in its actual concrete appearance is never the mechanical reflection of historical necessity, nor is it the result of some sort of chance (or subjective) mistake. It is rather the result of social conflicts, of social struggles, and of battles between forces representing opposing interests.

The predominance of the over-centralised system of economic management was itself the result of a concrete historical situation, in which different social interests and aims were to be found in conflict. In order to strengthen the power of the hierarchically structured administration which was untouched by social control, Stalin created an exceptionally convenient ideological justification for it. In his theory he presented the given form of over-centralised administration as an absolute ideal, and thus made it appear as some sort of final stage in the development of society, a stage which in all respects perfectly realised the aims of a socialist society.

Hierarchisation and standardisation

Stalin's theory about one-man responsibility in management, which was the most important ideological expression of over-centralised economic management, did not give a satisfactorily realistic answer to the question as to whom the one-man manager is responsible to. On an ideological level the answer seemed very simple indeed: "to the party", "to society". However, the question of who or which group creates social control remained an open one. Solutions were developed for different levels of management, but these differed in many respects from each other: (a) at the lower levels of economic management, unambiguously hierarchical administration prevailed—the wish of the higher administrative organ was decisive, and compared to it the local party and social organisations played a completely subordinate role; (b) in the higher organs, however, the hierarchical structure of the administration was made merely formal by party supervision which established a political control over management—that is, a control that was neither professional nor directly social.

The development of the management system of the socialist economy towards professionalisation, though it manifests itself in many forms, primarily means that a strong hierarchical order develops, especially at local levels, and this often makes all kinds of social supervision purely formal. In such cases a feeling of responsibility only develops and only exists in relation to the higher organs. Important decisions, such as changes in the managing personnel for example, are taken within this hierarchically structured system and in the institutions of party supervision connected with it. With a few rare exceptions, the society "outside" is unable to exercise any sort of influence over these decisions. In the socialist societies this hierarchisation extends not only to the sphere of state administration in the narrow sense, i.e. the management of state enterprises, but to the co-operative sector as well. In many cases the membership of a production co-operative freely elects its management only in the most formal sense, since in reality this decision is completely integrated into the hierarchical, bureaucratic order of the agricultural administration. In other words, the decision as to who will be made chairman of the co-operative is often in fact made by the district or county agricultural organs.

After hierarchisation, the next notable characteristic of a special apparatus which is separated from society and made responsible for the function of economic management is a greater degree of standardisation and stipulation of economic decisions and activities.

When analysing the advantages of the bureaucratic management of the economy over the traditional one, Max Weber drew his conclusions to no small extent from this tendency, which he saw as a necessary one. Although this phenomenon is certainly efficient within certain limits, it is nevertheless one of the natural barriers to the strengthening of the social character of administration, and to the "rehumanisation" of social management. The increase in stipulations strengthens bureaucratic relations (in the marxist sense) in the administrative apparatus, relations which are founded chiefly on the monopoly of professional knowledge itself. In this way an indispensable stratum of experts is created who are able to interpret the regulations.

Of course, neither the hierarchisation of the administration, nor the standardisation of decision-making processes which occurs within it, can be considered as bad in any absolute sense. Both are equally necessary phenomena, and are natural concomitants of the development of administrative organisations which have to a greater or lesser extent become separated from society as a result of the division of labour. But both hierarchisation and standardisation can develop to an unhealthy degree. This is not the only process that has negative consequences, with those institutions that serve to realise social control (that is, the various forms of party and social supervision) being pushed into the background. Such consequences can also arise from the pursuit of optimisation.

The acceleration of the development of the forces of production in recent years, even under capitalism, raises the question of whether it is possible to find an optimal degree of hierarchy and standardisation for the organisation which manages the economy. Going beyond this level would mean incurring serious material losses and in the final analysis a drop in efficiency, because it would make the organisation too rigid and hinder its adjustment to rapidly changing conditions. If we want to describe the development of the management system from this point of view, then simplifying the question, we can distinguish three stages or developmental tendencies: (a) in the initial phase of the development of industry a traditional management system developed; decisions were not stipulated from above, and hierarchy was only developed to a low degree; (b) as a result of the large-scale concentration of the forces of production, big production units came into being in which decisions increasingly became regulated from above, a strong hierarchical order developed, and direct orders became the most important means of management; (c) the acceleration of the rate of development of the forces of production demands a greater degree of flexibility, regulations and hierarchical order gradually become fetters on development, and it becomes necessary for certain units, which are now built into bigger organisational systems, to grow more autonomous once again. Of course these tendencies are not historical periods which follow one upon the other. Indeed, they can even come to prominence simultaneously, since the degree of development of the forces of production, and of the organisations of production, is very different in the different branches of the economy.

The predominance of the state administrative (étatist) principle in economic management

In the first period of socialist development the étatist principle came to prevail in economic management virtually down to the level of the foreman. Greater emphasis came to be placed on keeping the rules (including the orders of the plan) than on social interests or even economic results. In this way arose the now well-known phenomenon of the fetishisation of indices. Complete implementation of the central will, and adherence to the large number of ordinances and regulations, became the most important requirements. This, however, both necessarily pushed individual initiative into the background, and also made all attempts to estab-

40

lish social supervision purely formal.

The much-proclaimed, dogmatically rigidified and unquestionable social interest was seen as a justification for almost anything, and the upper levels of economic management presented themselves as the sole organs qualified to express and represent it. The proposition that, in certain cases, a "particular self-interest" could replace the general interest as the main motivation behind decisions was excluded in advance. This exclusion in itself increased the difference between the presumed and the real social interest, a difference which frequently arises where economic knowledge is limited.

In these years, the characteristic ideology for the justification of the étatist principle of economic management was developed. In this ideology, the submission of almost every field of economic management to the centralised and hierarchically structured state management was put forward as an immutable characteristic of socialism. If we were to search for the social roots of the dogmatic distortion of the marxist way of looking at society that developed in this period, we need scarcely look further than this ideology, which sought to preserve and more or less faithfully reflect the bureaucratic relations of the socialist state. To what extent its development was a historical necessity and to what degree it played a positive role in the various stages of historical development are separate questions. In our judgement of these questions, we must guard against an unhistorical point of view which would judge the past in terms of demands that have matured in modern circumstances.

The pursuit of enterprise autonomy

In recent years in almost every socialist country we have been able to discern attempts to free the lower levels of economic management, and chiefly the management of the individual enterprise, from the fetters of over-centralisation. Even in theoretical studies it is increasingly rare to find references to the enterprise director as the state's first representative in the enterprise. He is considered rather as the manager of an enterprise which has at its disposal a greater or lesser degree of autonomy and responsibility. The different branches of the management of a socialist enterprise, the functions of which have changed significantly as a result of the economic reforms, seek to free themselves from any kind of control. Therefore in pursuit of their own particular interests, they

41

fight not only against the various forms of centralisation, but also against the idea of social control.

The desire of enterprise management to free itself from higher administrative organs has two aspects. On the one hand, as a managerial apparatus fulfilling its own tasks it demands more autonomy, that is to say, a more complete and a less controllable authority and decision-making jurisdiction. On the other hand, however, as the representative of a society that functions as the proprietor, it wants to operate with greater efficiency and thus, within certain limits at least, it acts in accordance with the interests of society as a whole. Thus the particular interest of the enterprise administration is raised to the level appropriate to this given period of historical development.

However positive the striving for independence of enterprise administration may be, it is still in no way directed towards the creation of social control. Nor is there any reason to believe that it will necessarily mean the strengthening of such control. With the increase in its jurisdiction the character of economic management certainly changes, but its bureaucratic nature is not destroyed. In fact the separation of administration from society may grow even wider. This depends on the degree to which, within both the economic and the professional management of the enterprise, possibilities exist for the development of its power, and for its autonomy and independence from the society "outside". Where it has come under social control, enterprise management constitutes only a potential bureaucracy. This appears as an attempt to create an independent situation and to enforce the real consequences of bureaucratic relations, but it is an attempt that cannot be realised.

The possibility of bureaucratic relations (in the marxist sense) predominating as real relations will necessarily continue to exist as long as the need remains for an administration separate from society or (and this amounts to the same thing) until the time comes when, from the point of view of the individual, any "given" work in general—and work performed within the administrative organisation in particular—loses its significance and becomes unimportant to him. Until we reach this condition we shall have to recognise that the administrative apparatus's attempt to achieve "autonomy" and a situation of independence will continue to manifest itself as a tendency which has an objective social basis, even if conscious forces (the party, for example) systematically oppose it with their own educational methods.

We generally meet with the following arguments in defence of the "autonomy" of management, and against the idea of social supervision: (a) that the various types of social control restrict the efficiency of management and encourage uneconomical activities; (b) that social control limits the role of expertise because it is incapable of comprehending the complicated mechanism of management.

Basing itself on these arguments, the ideology corresponding to the desire for independence and reflecting the specific interests of enterprise management appears to be expanding in two directions at one and the same time. In very many instances we come across an exaggeration of the importance of scientific planning and programmed decisions, while we simultaneously meet with an attitude that considers the incorporation of workers into management to be unworkable from any practical point of view.

We can discern in this group of problems the simultaneous appearance of two demands which seem to be mutually contradictory, and this makes it extremely difficult for us to arrive at a correct attitude. The development of the specialised knowledge needed for decision-making in economic management really is extremely important, and looking at it from the interests of society as a whole it hardly seems possible to overestimate it. However, the socialist development of society demands the socialisation of this increasingly complicated "science of administration".

New problems constantly arise and these result in an important expansion in the stock of knowledge necessary for management. The Central Committee of the Communist Party of Czechoslovakia has only recently announced: "We must overcome subjectivism in management activity, and management must make use of the results of the social sciences, primarily sociology and psychology."

But even here a lot depends on social coercion. Under socialism management is compelled, in no small manner by social supervision itself, to continually widen its knowledge and in this respect to attain a level in keeping with the requirements of the age. Thus it is as a result of actual social encouragement that the organs dealing with economic management acquire the specialised knowledge which is one of the main sources of their autonomy and separation from society. Experience shows that the administrative apparatus can establish and preserve its professional monopoly with exceptional ingenuity and by the most diverse methods. For this the maintenance of secrecy is necessary above all else, and the creation of an atmosphere which presents every formulation of opinion from "outside" as unwarranted, and as an assault upon effective work, regardless of whether it comes from the press or from the party organisation. One of the most typical methods of justifying bureaucratic relations was and still is to turn the importance of its special knowledge into an absolute good. This point of view, even though our circumstances are different, is simply an extension of that mystery about which Marx wrote in his *Critique of Hegel's "Philosophy of Law"*: "The general spirit of the bureaucracy is the *secret*, the mystery preserved within itself by the hierarchy and against the outside world by being a closed corporation."[10]

It seems that this same monopoly situation, based on special knowledge, is further strengthened by the development of the "science of administration". However, there is a certain amount of illusion in this. The continual development of special knowledge of the administration and the programming of decisions does not only give rise to the desire to intensify the monopoly. These developments can transform themselves into their opposites and advance the awareness of wider social groups. In my opinion, as administration becomes more specialised and professional, it actually leads to a situation in which the average educated member of society can more easily survey the whole. (Naturally, the level of education is itself in a process of change.) This process makes it worth supporting the advance of socialist development with all the strength at our disposal. Of course, this trend cannot emerge if special knowledge is monopolised, but only if the democratisation of public life develops in the true meaning of the term.

In considerations about the modernisation of the socialist management system, the development of a socialist entrepreneurial stratum is often put forward as the only solution which can (if given a free hand) allow a more dynamic development of socialist society to take place than has so far been the case. According to this ideology of the "socialist manager", the management of the enterprise (the socialist entrepreneur or entrepreneurs) should be given almost complete freedom within the given legal bounds. Economic life should then be built around the relationship which exists between the socialist entrepreneur, the "bank" representing the interest of the entire society, and the worker freely disposing of his labour power. This line of thought merits special attention because, in the sphere of theoretical generalisation, it openly expresses the opinion which the majority of those who want to preserve or even extend the bureaucratic relations of socialist administration themselves defend in practice—but which they package up in a great variety of enticing arguments (the defence of special knowledge, the importance of one-man management, etc.). The clear theoretical expression of these ideas makes the debate easier, and helps us to demonstrate how sharply the overemphasis on the demand for optimisation, and the neglect of humanisation, can come into opposition with the perspectives of socialist development.

An important argument in all attempts of this sort is to point out that the masses of the workers show no particular interest in taking part in economic management. This argument appears to be supported by certain facts of experience. Yugoslav, Polish and Czech sociological studies are published one after the other to confirm not only that workers in enterprises are very poorly informed about the management problems of their enterprise, but also that their interest and participation is minimal. Our own Hungarian investigations support these findings. However, these facts are only symptomatic of a particular stage of historical development. They are the direct result of the alienation which developed under capitalism, and of the fact that, at the present level of socialist development, it has not yet been possible to transcend the very powerful social causes of alienation (the division of labour in particular). None of this refutes the basic tenet of marxism according to which, as far as his essence is concerned, man is a universal being and his natural striving is for the rehumanisation of his social relations, and (among these) of his relation to work and to the administration of society. Because of his species characteristics, and to the extent that he retains and develops his human properties, man cannot acquiesce in being a "cog" in some incomprehensible social machine, nor in losing control over his own life and work, in becoming the unthinking implementer of commands, the simple mimic of "ready-made" behavioural models.

The role of the party and the trade unions in the creation of social control over economic management

Under socialism there are two socially organised forces above all which offer themselves in opposition to the development of economic management as an institution separated from society, and thus in opposition to the rapid growth and rigidification of bureaucratic relations. These bodies are the party and the trade unions, both of which press for a division of power within management and administration. Naturally, this endeavour can only be successful if the interest of the working class at a particular level (or the interest of the society as a whole) finds expression within these organisations. In this respect, a lengthy and prolonged struggle ensues, and in certain historical periods (for example, when the dogmatic viewpoint gains ascendancy) it takes shape only as an unrealised possibility. The fulfilment of the historical tasks of these organisations depends on many social circumstances. Among others it depends upon the degree to which the party's and the trade unions' own apparatuses (organisations which themselves are inevitably developing) are interlocked with the leading organs of the state and the economy. It also depends on the extent to which they consider their function to be the creation of social supervision and control of the administration, and the extent to which their work is restricted to helping to fulfil the tasks of the administration.

In the different periods of socialist development the functions of both the party and the social organisations have gone through significant changes. In the first period their activity was subordinated to strengthening the socialist state since, quite naturally, the most important problem for social progress was to establish the new state, and to defend the proletarian power from its internal and external enemies. In this period both party and trade union organisations alike considered support for the aims of the socialist state to be their almost exclusive task. They too accepted that the interests of society as a whole were embodied in these aims. Thus, and with no little justification, it seemed to be an attack on socialism even to raise the idea that the apparatus carrying out state administration might not in every case be considered the bearer of the interest of society as a whole, or that in certain relations it might even be expressing its own interests and aims: this despite the fact that, at a theoretical level, such ideas could not be doubted by a single marxist.

In our judgement of this question we cannot forget the concrete conditions in which the socialist states came into being (at least when speaking of those that have so far been established). In the Soviet Union, in the years following the victory of socialist society, the welding together of the trade unions and the state power, the so-called "statification of the trade unions", was regarded as an almost self-evident solution. Lenin, however, first rejected this policy as inopportune at the time, and later explained and argued that it was a theoretically inappropriate solution too.

In many respects a new situation was created with the successful

46

strengthening of the socialist state. It was natural that emphasis should now be placed on the humanisation of administration, even though the realisation of this necessity was, and to some extent is still today, hindered by two linked factors. One of these, the more temporary, is the ascendancy of dogmatism. The other, more durable, is the aggressive policies engendered by the environment of capitalism and imperialism.

The creation of new forms of social control

If we start out from the developmental trends of socialist society, then we must conclude that, however efficient and thus important the party and trade unions become in the creation of social control over management, they are nevertheless unable to provide a satisfactory solution. In addition to them, it appears to be necessary to construct some form of social control over economic administration, in which supervision is exercised by the members of society acting as owners, or at least by organs which represent them. Until now, the Parliament and the local councils have been the only institutions of this type. Large and important areas of economic life have, however, remained outside their sphere of influence: ministerially-directed industry and state agriculture, for example.

This problem was posed especially sharply after the economic reform. Before the reform, the strong hierarchical order that prevailed in this field appeared to make up for the absence of direct social supervision. The accomplishment of social supervision and direct social control over economic administration in fact comprises two sets of problems which can be separated out to a certain extent:

(1) The representation of the property rights of the members of society. Society, as the trustee of the property of the entire people, has the right to exercise supervision over the activity of economic management, and within this over the management of individual enterprises, not only through special administrative institutions but also, more directly, with the aid of its own social organs. It also has the right to judge the performance of this management.

(2) The enterprise and co-operative collectives, as well as the workers directly interested in the performance of the enterprises and co-operatives, have a right to exercise supervision over the activity of enterprise management, and to state opinions about it. Since the economic reform, this right has been substantiated by

47

the fact that the enterprise collectives are becoming to a much greater degree materially interested in the efficient performance of the enterprise.

It is in order to fulfil these functions that the supervisory boards have come into existence, even though the latest decision of the party's Central Committee directed that they should not be created everywhere. Their task will be the effective social supervision of the work of management on the basis of a complex evaluation of the performance of the enterprise. As well as being justified by many practical experiments, the basic ground for the creation of these institutions was provided by the theoretical consideration that at today's stage in the development of socialist society, the time is not ripe for the introduction of social self-management in state enterprises. Instead, a system of educated management must be created which will be extremely interested in the efficient performance of the enterprise, but which will also work alongside effective social supervision, on which it depends for its very existence. The realisation of this latter demand would be both a valid and a very important step towards the socialisation of management in contemporary Hungarian society.

The tasks of the enterprise supervisory boards are still the subject of heated debate. In my opinion, what must be stressed above all in their work is that they should exercise continuous supervision and that, on the basis of this, they should regularly provide systematic evaluations of the work of enterprise management. They should not, however, be given responsibility for making decisions concerning the future activity of the enterprise.

It is necessary to restrict categorically the responsibilities of the supervisory boards in this way because otherwise they would limit the jurisdiction of the enterprise managers, and take over a part of their responsibility. On the one hand, this would contribute to the establishment of a situation in which no one would actually bear responsibility for the activity of the enterprise. On the other hand, it would also weaken the activity of the supervisory board, since it would lead to a certain degree of fusion between the institutions of social supervision and those of management. This sort of interlocking can be clearly observed today between ministerial and enterprise management, and it is one of the greatest barriers to the efficient functioning of the ministries as organs of supervision. The most important task of the supervisory board should be to pass judgement, at least once a year, on the performance of the enterprise and particularly of its management, on the basis of experiences acquired over the year and of the director's reports and the balance sheets. This work should be based upon the results and developmental trends of the preceding three to five years, and the board should under no circumstances be allowed to base its judgements on comparisons made only between the current year and the preceding year, and least of all on comparisons with plans prepared by the enterprise itself.

The social nature of the enterprise supervisory boards, of course, does not only depend on the correct definition of their spheres of activity, but on their composition as well. One part of the board's members should be chosen by the members of the collective and with the participation of the trade unions. The professional managers of the enterprise, however, should not be eligible for election. The other part of the board should be drawn from experts who are independent of the management. In this way the danger of interlocking leadership can be avoided. An element deserving great attention in this latter respect is that special knowledge has a dominant role in this thoroughly social, that is to say non-bureaucratic, organ of administration. In this way, the greatest worry in relation to social supervision and control, the absence of special knowledge, disappears or at least is greatly reduced.

However many safeguards are worked out to prevent the enterprise supervisory boards from being deprived of all real power, and to prevent the particular interests of enterprise management from getting the upper hand, this possibility still remains a real danger. Indeed, the enterprise supervisory boards can only become effective social agencies in the course of the battle of social forces representing interests and aims which in many respects stand in opposition to one another. In this struggle the stakes are high.

We must remember that socialism is a more developed social condition than capitalism not simply because it can become a more dynamic system in an economic sense, but also because the abolition of private ownership of the means of production creates the possibility for the humanisation of social administration. Only the realisation of this dual possibility—dynamic economic progress and the development of humanised social relations—is capable of making socialism attractive in every respect for the workers of the more developed capitalist countries. On the other hand, in those societies which have already taken the socialist road of development, the realisation of this possibility renders unshakeable our conviction that the socialist system is a higher stage in the development of mankind than any preceding one, and the certain path to the "realm of freedom". This idea was expressed in the resolution of the Central Committee of the Hungarian Socialist

Workers' Party on "The Reform of the Economic System", where it was declared that these two principles "must be considered not as mutually exclusive but as mutually complementary principles within socialist relations".

IV: Scientific Research and the Management Apparatus

Scientific research has become one of the biggest "industries" of our times. In the developed industrial countries, the number of employees in this sector is by no means negligible. At the same time, scientific activity is playing an increasing role in shaping the trends of development in these countries, or to put it in its usual and simplified way, science is becoming a direct productive force. Its increasing scope and the changes in its function have raised new problems about the planning and organisation of this activity. The tasks of scientific activity can only be fulfilled in an appropriate institutional framework; they cannot be performed without their own special management apparatus, which is separated from research work. Traditional management, which was based directly on researchers, has necessarily been replaced in the scientific field by a special machinery for the administration and organisation of scientific work. This is only a part of a broader and more general process, a nationwide separation and hierarchisation of management and administrative functions. But there are many problems specific to it, which need thorough examination.

This change—the separation or professionalisation of the management of science or, to put it differently and without malice, its bureaucratisation—involves a host of sociological problems; the most important of these are the ones which stem from the contradiction between the aims of independent management and administration on the one hand, and the inner characteristics of the research activities themselves on the other hand. It is impossible to understand the sociological problems of research management by ignoring the typical forms of this contradiction and simply concentrating instead on (for example) measuring how research workers utilise their time, or on using sociometrical methods to examine the sympathies and antipathies which arise in "team work". This primitive type of empirical sociology is outdated even in the Western countries. If we want to leave it behind us then we must begin by analysing the contradictions, typical of the present level of scientific research, between the inner characteristics of scientific activity and the management of it by a historically necessary special machinery (bureaucratised management

51

in the Weberian sense). This interrelation is typified by the following specific contradictions:

(1) While scientific work actually yields a relatively high degree of independence and makes a high degree of self-supervision both possible and requisite, management seeks to restrict or at least regulate this independence for some institutional purpose. In fact, scientific activities cannot be restricted to institutional frameworks or even national ones: this is a thesis which is currently accepted not only by marxists (this is worth stressing at times and places in which nationalism is on the upsurge), but also by every scientist committed to the cause of social and scientific progress. At the same time, management imposes not only national but also much narrowed institutional restrictions on scientific activities, thus emphasising certain particular interests.

(2) While scientific work requires a continuous development of human approaches and abilities which perhaps take a long time to result in actual achievements, management cares either about achievements alone (if it is pursuing rational aims) or else about hierarchical division. Alexander Szalai is right in saying that "research work 'in the making' is a scarcely noticeable process: it partly goes on in human minds, often after working hours, at indefinable moments, in a state of semi-consciousness or in inexpressible ideas, and it partly consists of a multitude of mechanical activities, behavioural motives and elements not specifically characteristic of research work whose function in the research process cannot be easily estimated before the result is known, and cannot be properly reconstructed afterwards".[11] Some psychologists even raise doubts about whether scientific research is always work, since accidents, "eureka" experiences and "inspiration" undoubtedly play a large role, even if clarifying what the problem is requires long preparatory work. It is worth quoting S. L. Rubinshtein here, who wrote that "inspiration is in most cases a culminating point in the concentration of our extraordinarily highly-geared intellectual and physical efforts which, after a certain interval, encapsulate the results of long, arduous, concentrated work".[12]

(3) In scientific work, in spite of the increasing differentiation and division of labour, a greater importance is correspondingly attached to communication, and whatever the inner logic of scientific development, individual abilities still play a large role. The management of scientific work, however, sticks to its taylorist traditions and, under the influence of pure rationalism, seeks "from outside" to determine how work should be divided and inter-

52

related. In scientific co-operation, the exchange of activities is not determined by commercial considerations, nor even by the technical division of labour, but by the inner logic of the development of the various branches of science. And because this involves an interrelation among sciences in which the mediation of the means of production is of little importance, the subjective factor naturally plays an important role. Because of this contradiction, there are potential conflicts even in cases where management allows a great deal of freedom of action to scientific research—e.g. in the abolition of fixed working hours, or in the large amount of consideration given to individual approaches and abilities in drafting plans. If management does not show this kind of flexibility, then conflict between management and scientific research is an everyday occurrence. This contradiction increases if management tries to classify scientific research within a particular sphere into functional sections or "departments" in accordance with traditional management methods, and gives these priority over groups working on ad hoc themes. This whole contradiction forms one of the most fundamental sets of organisational alternatives for the management of science.

(4) Scientific work is not measured directly in practice, and therefore the evaluation of its social usefulness is incomparably more difficult than that of any other activities. Because of this, researchers may be more easily drawn to overestimate the importance of their own work than those whose achievements can be directly measured in practice (this applies not only to manual workers but also to professionals such as doctors, technical engineers, agronomists, etc.). But no matter how difficult the task is, management cannot give up its evaluating function, for as I shall try to demonstrate later, perhaps one of the most important reasons for its existence is that it can distinguish the important from the less important and thus, on the basis of well-founded analytic and objective viewpoints, it can give priority to certain researchers and research trends over others.

(5) The management of science does not expect the scientific researcher to be an independent creator, but to identify himself with the aims of the enterprise or institution, and to utilise and develop his knowledge in its interests. In the long term, however, better results are obtained from those researchers who are oriented towards their own scientific activities than from those who identify themselves primarily with institutional aims.

All these contradictions can be easily observed in practice. To those whose thinking is mechanical (who on both sides of the argument are unfortunately not a rare breed), this means that the solution lies in liquidating one side of the contradiction or the other. The conflict between the activities of management and the imminent characteristics of scientific work is illustrated by the vehemence of the opinion expressed by the chief executive of a big American pharmaceutical factory: "If we want to be competitive, we cannot exist without research. I have a burning desire to solve these problems without engaging scientific experts. We have to spend twice as much time on the problems of the scientists at our research and development departments as we do on the problems of all the other employees put together." At the same time, the representatives of the scientific world are unsparing in their accusations against management, and the main and most frequently repeated accusation being about the restriction or even extermination of creative abilities. If we wish to avoid either of these two extremes, then it is not enough simply to tolerate those tendencies which enable research to resist the aims of management by means of their "inner", immanent characteristics; we must also be aware of the social necessity which makes the development of management as an independent function inevitable.

Functions of management in scientific research

In order to find a basis for accepting the necessity of a specialised management apparatus, we must first of all review all the functions which at certain stages of development have demanded the establishment of a machinery dealing exclusively with administrative tasks. It seems to me necessary to distinguish the three following tasks.

(1) Management methods are required first of all for the creation of an appropriate "preference" system, for deciding the priorities among the various research trends and establishments, i.e. it is necessary to distinguish between socially and institutionally motivated research. In fact this kind of "preference" is the essential motive of scientific planning: the task is not to set certain aims, but to determine what backing can be given to the scientifically established aims of research on the basis of a deep overall analysis of social expediency. I have already tried to show that this is a very complicated function, chiefly because in the "established" evaluation there are no unambiguously defined criteria with which to select the objective priority. Because of this, difficulties arise not only when the interests involved are those of some capitalist

grouping, but also when it is the aim of a socialist society based on socialist property relations, or of some state enterprise or institution. In the industrialised societies (both capitalist and socialist), an ever-increasing proportion of the national income is allotted to scientific research, and therefore the expedient or "optimal" distribution of these funds presents more and more of a problem. The task of distribution, at least at a higher stage of development, cannot be entrusted to the research workers alone, since the scientific researcher who identifies himself with his work to a high degree cannot be expected to show the required "objectivity" appropriate to the interests of society or of some institution.

(2) Management seeks to justify its existence mostly by its co-ordinating activities, which largely consist of the apparently rational task of eliminating "parallelisms". But this seemingly sound argument can lead to an orientation which is in many respects unsound. To understand this, one first of all has to query the task itself, the basic task of co-ordination and of eliminating "parallelisms". The co-ordination of scientific activities on one particular level can be executed only by relying upon its "internal" forces, since the prerequisite knowledge of the partial processes which have to be linked together is usually missing to the "outside" observer, and the often intricate network of individual relations usually remains unknown territory. While management "from outside" is virtually powerless to co-ordinate research carried out on one particular level, the link between research and practice cannot be established without an effective contribution from management. If research workers are expected to fulfil this linking function, not only will they be taken away from their own basic tasks, but also this very important function will itself be at risk, since the transfer of research results to the realm of practice requires specific knowledge, abilities and experience. This means that a management apparatus in the sphere of science appears as a necessity wherever the creation of a *direct link* between research and practice is especially important, that is to say especially in the field of technological research, whereas the traditional methods of directing scientific research can be preserved where this link is less important. It is relevant at this point to mention briefly the frequent problem of parallel research, which usually appears in the ideology of those in management who are on the side of centralism. The elimination of "parallelisms" is not an immediate necessity even in the field of production, because the monopolistic trends which result from it often cause incomparably more harm than parallelism itself. Its usefulness is still more questionable in scien-

tific work, where important successes achieved in one scientific field are often the direct consequence of the advantages of parallelism: for example, the possibility of close communications, continuous scientific cross-checking, competition, etc.

(3) There is one other historically established function of management which requires attention. This is the continuous maintenance of the technical conditions of research work, and the organisation of those technical services which are needed immediately. Scientific institutions, especially in technological fields, become "workshops", whose research efficiency can be considerably increased by appropriate organisation of the technical services. Of course we must be careful not to jump to hasty conclusions. The organisational, institutional concentration of research (its "industrialisation") will not always bring more results. As in the field of production, an optimal measure of concentration can be found; management's attempt to bring about greater concentration is almost natural, while the research workers themselves show a greater preference for working in smaller "workshops".

Structural disorders in management

I have stressed the historical necessity of the emergence of management, but I do not intend to give the impression that by developing some kind of clever, "expert" management we can eliminate the contradiction between management and the immanent qualities of scientific research activities. The conflicts which stem from the objective relations may well sharpen if management takes over superfluous functions for the sake of strengthening its power, or if it ignores the inner qualities of scientific work. On the other hand, a sharpening of the conflict can be avoided, and the efficacy of the research can be considerably aided by management, if an appropriate form can be found for the movement of the conflict.

Sociology, however, has never been interested in the accidental shortcomings of the management of science, but only in those shortcomings which are its necessary consequences, i.e. which spring from a given structure. These shortcomings and dangers are as follows.

(1) One of the main dangers is that the achievement principle will be overshadowed by the status principle. A special management apparatus is always hierarchical, and by its nature it strives for a distribution of individual wages and prestige according to the relations of dependence. In scientific work, however, this kind

of distribution of wages and prestige necessarily conflicts with its actual achievements, since it gives the activities of research workers an approximately identical character. Often research workers do not try to obtain promotion to managerial, administrative or planning posts, and very often they also lack the abilities and skills needed for such posts. If management were to accept the achievement principle (which is also an important precondition of its own efficiency), then it would be acting in accordance with its own nature and with the object of its activities, as opposed to accepting some principle outside its own framework. However, this is a difficult requirement to fulfil, since the administrative staff usually rank their own activities higher than they should, and therefore they consider it fair that they should have a higher share of the institutional advantages in every respect. Many people expect the achievement principle to be brought about as a result of the increase in trading at the outset of the new economic reform. This, however, is a dangerous illusion (and "illusion" is too kind a term for a value system which is based on market criteria). In fact, the materialisation of scientific work, its appearance as a use-value, presupposes a high degree of intermediacy and a long time-lag. This makes the mechanical application of market criteria impossible, and correspondingly demands that the priorities selected by management be based upon thorough analysis.

(2) Another big danger to the efficacy of scientific work that is due to structural causes is the "prescribedness" of human activities, and the exaggerated importance of this. As Max Weber pointed out in his excellent analysis, in order to promote the efficiency of management there is a great need for "prescribedness" (standardisation), and people in the various posts must submit their activities to the prescribed regulations. However, without wishing to give this matter a pejorative slant, I would say that this requires a conformist attitude, and that this conformity is often held up to be a most valuable human feature in management. The problem starts at school, where (as the relevant literature so often shows) teachers have a higher opinion of amenable pupils than of non-conformists. They try to "break in" the strong "individualists". Management adopts a similar function and often fulfils it successfully, although this success can only be achieved at the expense of creative abilities. Eugene Randsepp, describing conditions in the U.S.A., has correctly observed that "no other factor would have brought about such a decline in creative abilities as the sanctioning of conformism. Conformism is regarded not only as a safe and secure way of life, but also as a correct and desirable attitude."[13] At the same

57

time, conformism has a certain rationality for management, even when its distorting influence upon individuality is by no means small. In the case of scientific research workers, however, it is not only harmful to individuals but inevitably reduces the efficacy of creative work too, because scientific activities, as I have already pointed out, are by their essence impossible to standardise. In order to achieve results, it is not conformism that is needed but the opposite: a strictly critical attitude, disputing everything that has existed and been achieved up to that point.

(3) Finally, I wish to deal with something that cannot be regarded as an isolated or rare occurrence: the kind of distortion of the value system in management when certain administrative functions become independent of the original aim and, instead of striving for the *increased efficacy* of research activities, become an end in themselves. The institutional interests in this kind of case are caught in a vice: on the one hand there is the representative of management, who sees management as an end in itself and who therefore realises the institutional interests in a formal sense, and on the other hand there is the research worker, who identifies himself with scientific development and grumbles against management even when it represents its own institutional aims cleverly and with the necessary tolerance. In order to escape this danger, the management must be at its best; it must acknowledge the priority of research activities over its own function, i.e. it must regard it as a basic task to give overall support to scientific research, and to supply it with the required technical conditions. This distortion in the value system of management occurs especially when the institutional aims are manifested in an ambiguous way, when its supervisory organs expect the institution to provide not so much effective research activity as the maintenance of "formal" order, the avoidance of all conflicts and disturbing elements. In this case it follows almost naturally that the administrative aim ranks itself higher than the research itself, and considers it a tremendous injustice if research activities enjoy higher social prestige and, *horribile dictu*, greater financial recognition; the nature of the special management apparatus is such that it makes every effort it can to redress this "injustice". This kind of disorder in management in Hungary is a potential one rather than a genuine symptom, partly because specialised management is not so well developed here. The management of science has retained many traditional elements which more or less prevent the negative tendencies from making headway.

Of course, the possibility that the negative factors mentioned above may develop does not justify our denying the expediency of having a special management apparatus, since the latter will appear inevitably anyway, as a social necessity, and in the final analysis it promotes the further development of science. But as in many other fields of social life, progress has its price, and the more we try to ignore it, the more we have to pay.

V: Alternatives of Social Development

Social development can move in any one of several directions, including dead ends. We have to choose from among possibilities, whether we want to or not; and it is in this that our freedom as well as our responsibility lies.

If we are to make choice easier by working out the implications from an informed sociological viewpoint, then what is needed above all is a realistic analysis of European socialism up to the present day. The internal critique which has developed in just the last fifteen years in the socialist countries has made its contribution towards this; it may not in any way have produced satisfactory solutions to the problems which have arisen, but it has nonetheless focused attention on some considerations of great importance for the future, even though further discussion, at least about the details, will be necessary.

Through the historical experience of socialism over a century and a half we have come to understand a great many things; however, we have by no means yet fully considered all the essential conclusions to be drawn from this experience. Our times have shown without a doubt that marxism—whose most significant characteristic is its ability to bring about change in society by working through the various alternative routes progress can take —is most threatened by the emergence of "national marxism", in which the original internationalism of the sociological and ideological aims are lost. The latter then becomes no more than an empty slogan, one in fact which the national ideology not only fails to support but at every turn prevents from being carried out. It is inevitable, therefore, that this "national marxism" loses its ability to work through the alternatives open to progress, and cannot help becoming an apologia for whatever solution has already developed in the country concerned. Nowadays, national marxism and this "apologetic" marxism are synonymous.

What complicates the situation and makes it more difficult to recognise is the fact that originally it was precisely the development of the national forms (or more broadly the national characteristics) which was hindered, because the defence of the already developed forms was dogmatically identified with the defence of socialism, with the result that this attitude appeared to be a sort of supreme internationalism. These days, however, it is no longer considered so "internationalist" to defend the already developed forms to such an extent, since national characteristics in the social countries, as a result of various sociological and historical forces that have come into play, have irresistibly forced their way forward, and every country has come up with a different answer to the crucial question of how society should be organised.

It has to be accepted as an established historical fact that the socialist system of society is here to stay, but also that there exist roads to socialist development which differ from one another in several respects. Their existence itself is undeniable proof that there cannot be one sole form of world progress which is socialist (in other words, which abolishes private ownership of the means of production). If, however, the "official" marxism that develops in a particular country does not treat the forms resulting from its own practical solutions as simply possible alternatives, but regards them as absolute, the *only* socialist possibility, then it becomes enslaved by forms, instead of taking the essentials as its starting-point, and shows that it is incapable of providing a theory for truly revolutionary practice.

Historical precedent and the influence of rigid ideology make it more likely that this danger will become a reality; certain institutions and social conditions have seemed to be specifically identified with and characteristic of the classic road to socialism, with the result that there appeared to be *only one* historically possible alternative. Not only has this assumption hampered the development of marxism as a theory of revolutionary practice, it has also held back the marxist social sciences (economics, sociology) which, by questioning the conclusions reached in their areas, would have made it their job to work out the implications of possible alternatives for the future.

However, the situation is more complex still, since only those social sciences committed to progress—concerned not with power politics but with the historical situation—can play an active part in working out realistic ways to progress. The theory of revolutionary practice can be helped by the social sciences only if they can to a certain degree provide a view "from outside" of how society must evolve—regardless of the forms already developed—and can commit themselves to the cause of social progress rather than to some given solution.

It is in this and only this sense that a significant role can be played by the development of a marxist sociology. If such a sociology can develop, supported by the body of knowledge that exists in marxist philosophy, and if it makes use of the results that can today be obtained in analysing society (the different methods of information-collecting, structural analysis, cybernetics and computer science, statistics, etc.), then it can provide data on which revolutionary practice can rely, not only with regard to the present day, but also about the social effects that may be expected in the future as a result of the different possibilities of development.

Marxist philosophy too, of course, if it is to fulfil its function of advancing social development, must concern itself with the principal alternatives of development. In other words, the main tendencies of marxist philosophy are linked not only with the very general questions of social development—the confirmation or denial of which give rise to possible support or rejection of other potential avenues of development—but are also inevitably connected to the actual alternatives themselves, as practical objectives for social action. Even so, philosophy may temporarily still treat these questions on an abstract level; individual works, or even life-works, can be valuable without being considered in direct connection with specific alternatives for development.

So far as philosophy is concerned, the dilemma of being limited by historical or specific political situations does not, at least for a while, necessarily result in conflict, as it usually does for the social sciences, whose fundamental purpose is to analyse the historic alternatives by using an approved system of values worked out by some philosophical tendency, and to make a direct contribution to the way in which new development possibilities are concretely formulated.

From this it follows that in order for marxist philosophy to serve really practical ends it requires assistance from the concrete social sciences. A classic example of this is the way in which Marx not only made use of the economic science of his period, creating a marxist school of political economy, but also managed to put to good use in his analyses the reports of factory inspectors—the equivalent of modern sociological research. It is imperative that marxist philosophy, as much as sociology, gets to the point of making concrete social analyses and of taking up a position on the various development alternatives, in order to progress beyond the defensive, dogmatic phase without getting stuck in some kind of moralising.

The full significance of this critical stage faces us today, for the various possible roads for socialist development have not merely been formulated but in fact have already clashed; and anyone who is wholeheartedly committed to the cause of social progress can, indeed must, make a choice. No longer is it a case of advocates of progress in the European socialist countries having only one alternative: either to preserve the achievements of socialism, or to return to capitalism.

Hungary provides a convincing example of this. The choice between two possible variants of the economic system has evolved into a formula: either a system of planning and directives, or a market mechanism regulated by planning. This formulation is mainly significant because of what it reveals about method, and because it leads the way toward deliberate change in other areas of social life.

The attitude taken today by marxism towards the nature of the power structure, i.e. executive power or (more precisely) the administration of society, and towards the theoretical, partly practical alternatives, is its greatest problem. Although it may be possible to ignore the subject for a time, society ever more urgently needs some practical action. There are currently three, perhaps four, possibilities open to us: administration by experts representing the interests of the totality, in which individual aims and interests are out of the question, or at the very least are considered to be definite subjective failings; the administration of society by itself, in which however the disadvantages of domination by bureaucracy, administration by experts, have not yet been overcome; administration by experts with their own interests and aims, accepted as a social necessity, but over which there can and must be some social control to prevent the development of a bureaucratic power without limits; and finally, the reign of bureaucracy and technocracy—which is also a possibility, though I do not consider that as a solution it would meet the basic aims of socialist development, and therefore I shall not discuss it in particular.

Administration by experts representing the interests of the whole of society, as the first alternative

This is of course not the first time that marxist sociological analysis has focused a great deal of attention on the fact that socialism has succeeded in what were previously backward agrarian societies, or at least societies with agrarian policies, particularly in situations where the economy was in a run-down state after war. Subsequently, economic problems came to the fore, almost as if by a natural law; and it went almost without saying that the economic

63

goal was to attain the level of the developed industrial societies, even though the actual plans were quite unrealistic. There were those, for example, who imagined that the disadvantages of decades could be made good within a few short years by applying the advantages of socialism.

Not surprisingly, this historical situation brought about a state of affairs where, because the best possible results were insisted upon, the problem of humanisation, of creating a human social context, was forced into the background. And one can only wonder that some people—including even some of those who call themselves marxist philosophers—are still trying to justify and to perpetuate this situation, explaining how the acceleration of economic development will in itself bring about the humanisation of social conditions.

This was how, in the twenties in the Soviet Union, in the midst of passionate debates and social strife, when economic goals and accumulation were supreme, the first alternative for administering socialist society developed. According to this, an administrative apparatus had to be formed and stabilised, but it could not be a vehicle for bureaucracy since it was responsible for the interests of society as a whole (particularly that of rapid economic growth) and had no aims or interests of its own. It became almost a cliché to observe, as is often still done today, and in Hungary, that "under socialism, every state organ is carrying out the people's interests, since the workers are in power."

The activities of the Communist Party appeared to provide the main proof of this theory, for not only did it conduct the administration of all levels of society but also acted as a watchdog over it; it both limited and shared the power of the administration at the same time. This means that any action opposed to the officially declared interests of the state was sabotage, or at the least a subjective mistake, and had no structural causes. The creation of strict party control followed naturally from this, as did the development of a state security police force much more extensive than the interests of state security justified. This was the social background which made it possible for the big trials to take place, though it by no means justified any need for them.

Even the strictest system of supervision, however, cannot solve the structural problems while they are being treated as subjective offences and defects. Up to now the experience of the European socialist countries has demonstrated almost without exception that although society can get along without private ownership, it still cannot do away with a special administration that has its own aims and interests and is separate from society—a bureaucracy, in marxist terms; if it does, it has in the end to rebuild it in one way or another, whether it wants to or not. The administrative apparatus must be firmly established and must be made interested in its own workings, even if that makes a whole series of social anomalies inevitable and leads to phenomena that are anything but fitting to the image of future socialism. In practice this is more or less taken into account nowadays, even where theses are put forward for keeping the old conception unchanged in the face of all the facts, i.e. the refusal to admit that administrative apparatuses inevitably have interests and aims of their own which they are in a position to enforce, because of the very real power which their functions afford them.

Within the administrative apparatus, changes have taken place that have further deepened the rift between the ideology, which considers the interests of the entire community to be vested in the administration, and the actual situation.

The administrative stratum which has evolved in socialist Europe can be identified as three essentially different social groups, whose importance in relation to each other has altered considerably compared with the original conditions.

(a) The group of people who had taken part in the communist workers' movement became a very important constituent element at the time when the leading circle developed; to differing extents and in different historical situations—both in the legal and the illegal movements—they had all participated in the movement's experiences. A large proportion of them were workers, employees living on wages or salaries. This stratum alone embodied "political dependability" and had as its dominant concept an opposition to the development of any sort of hierarchy. It would be necessary to undertake a special study in order to determine how their social role was influenced by the "trials"—in which some were the accusers, some the accused. Unquestionably, the attack was the consequence of mounting distrust and of the increasing demand for professional skills.

(b) The "technocracy", meanwhile, had appeared on the stage of history, comprising the old guard of experts carried over from the former system of the capitalist order but also the technical intelligentsia brought up by socialism itself. The entry of the latter is spectacular, for they are taking over more and more positions. The objection cannot be raised against them that they are politically unreliable, for of course in most cases they have no political views; but at the same time they are well-versed in technical matters and are familiar with the increasingly complicated technical and general questions in their specialised fields. The most characteristic thing about them perhaps is that they have no ideology of their own; they have borrowed a great deal from the preceding group but are also strongly influenced by the West.

The experts first appear as indispensable advisers of the first substratum, which developed out of the workers' movement, and later became rivals for filling practically every position of control.

(c) While the often spectacular struggle between the "factions from the movement" and the "technical intelligentsia" continues, a third character comes on the scene and makes off with the prize: the "socialist manager" substratum. This particular type is not a "man of the workers' movement" nor yet simply a "technical man"—although he may be recruited from either of these substrata—but a specialist in management, in setting up an enterprise. For a time it may perhaps be an advantage to him to have been part of the workers' movement and to possess technical knowledge, but this is almost irrelevant if in his "bureaucratic career" he proves himself to be capable of putting into practice his management flair. This requires several characteristics, some of which society considers positive, some negative. A striving for rationalism is the basic feature of his ideology, but what characterises his methods of management is an endeavour to be efficient at all costs.

The amalgamation of the three substrata, each supported by a different life-style more or less independently of "where they come from", results in the stable management stratum which in almost every branch of society today controls management; and, what is more, it functions in significantly more refined and effective ways than at early stages in its evolvement.

This development cannot be understood, however convenient it might be to try, without a historical analysis of the role of the communist workers' parties. Such parties and movements, when they come to power (and when the authority for controlling and decision-making at various levels is centralised) not only limit and share the power of management but are also capable, at least to a certain extent, of reducing its negative aspects. The heads of enterprises and institutions have to account for their work to local party organisations whose members enjoy equal rights, whatever their job. This work can thus be assessed by party members, and general resolutions can be passed on it. The local party organisations, as a result of these rights, are able to limit the personal dependence that can easily develop in a relationship of leader and led. Alternatively they can restrict its harmful effects through to

66

some extent breaking down the rigid hierarchy that arises from the division of labour.

A new problem, however, also made its appearance in the internal life of the parties which had gained power, making its existence obvious in several ways. It had for decades been noticed that the number of direct producers and service workers in the communist workers' parties of the European socialist countries had been stagnating, even gradually falling. In the years following the development of the socialist state it was possible to regard this as a natural phenomenon requiring no explanation, for of course during that period thousands of the "old" members of the workers' movement were going over into the administrative systems—state, economic, military, etc.—and that obviously meant a considerable reduction of the percentage of direct producers and service workers in the party. However, this still did not explain how, as later happened, the number of party members, while growing, reflected a decreasing number of direct producers and service workers with the emphasis instead being transferred to workers in the administration, or more generally to those pursuing intellectual occupations. This always seemed, from the point of view of the dominant ideology, to be an anomaly, an unhealthy phenomenon, and an almost constant battle was waged against it; yet, I might add, this only rarely and fleetingly brought even a technical result.

It seemed to us at the beginning of the fifties that this unwelcome development in the party's composition was attributable to subjective errors on the part of the lower ranks of party leaders. At first the leadership did fight against this phenomenon and even made use of criminal law and other administrative procedures to this end. For instance, during that time there was a case in which we expelled the first secretary of a provincial party council from the party on a charge of excluding manual workers from the party. It literally did not occur to us that the cause of this phenomenon, which was felt throughout the country, might be structural.

However, as time passed, it was natural that the recalcitrance of the process which one sought to suppress began to induce doubt in the functionaries themselves. A line of thinking developed which, adopting the ideology of bureaucratic management, came to consider the decreased participation of the direct producer in the composition of party membership and in the activities of the society almost a natural development, and regarded it as a direct consequence of the cultural difference between intellectual and manual workers. To this way of thinking, "those in the adminis-

67

tration are 'more cultured' and it is therefore quite natural that they should participate in greater numbers in the party than the 'backward' strata of manual workers." (This belief, never formulated in writing in Hungary, but emphasised more by word of mouth, is assumed to refer particularly to the manual labourers of the co-operative farms.)

The problem of organisation is neither a subjective error nor can it simply be put down to cultural differences between the various strata; an entirely different kind of social phenomenon lies behind it. Before I explain this, however, let us review the other likely alternatives for society's power structure and also for the position of the party.

Self-management as a historically new social alternative

If we are now to define our attitude to the future development of socialism, it is absolutely essential to review, without prejudice or illusion, the experience of Yugoslavia since 1948. In Yugoslavia, a new type of power structure for a socialist society came into being which unquestionably appeared as the historical negation of a power structure characterised by centralised management, and, at the same time, as a new and historically feasible alternative direction for socialist development. It may be that it is precisely this set of problems which most demands that marxist social science in the socialist countries—in Yugoslavia and elsewhere—free itself from current national political and power situations, and begin a realistic analysis of the historical position.

The theory and practice of social self-management developed out of a rejection of the type of management that claimed to represent the interests of society as a whole, and it takes as its starting point the thesis that management is inevitably bureaucratic. This leads it to see the changeover to social self-management as the only socialist solution. This disavowal embodies both the historical significance and the limitation of the new alternative. What the introduction of this system of self-management aimed at was an end to "bureaucratic centralism", an end to the separation of authority and power by transferring to "workers' communities" the power that goes with the governing of society and management. This solution did not explicitly deny the need to build up a cultured and effective management, but in practice this as an aim completely lost its importance; and if we still nevertheless see progress being made in this area, it is far more the result of spon-

68

taneous social forces than of deliberate effort.

In the previous solution, the communist parties saw their primary and immediate tasks as being to build up management apparatuses, to supervise their work and in this way to increase the efficiency of society; but the Yugoslav League of Communists "regarded it as its chief task to educate the workers to manage themselves in their own interest and in the interest of the socialist community." As a result, two opposing concepts of the party's function had developed which were to become one of the central themes for political discussion in the last decade.

The working out of the theory of social self-management, using Marx's concept of social development, and the course set towards carrying it out in practice, have already provided extremely valuable experiences for the whole international workers' movement. They have above all questioned irrevocably the validity of the assertion that the management systems that evolve in socialism are in the interests of the whole of society, and that consequently a bureaucratic condition is naturally incapable of developing within socialism. From the point of view of the fight against bureaucracy, however, self-management does not show itself to be completely effective; for in spite of this theory, management does need to develop, and in fact it is almost inevitable that it can and does include bureaucratic, technocratic and political elements, and it may attain real power "behind the scenes", under the guise of self-managed institutions. It is for these reasons that the struggle against bureaucracy becomes an extremely complex affair.

It is not easy to say what stage this process of building a separate management has reached in Yugoslavia today, where the practice of "self-management" has had the longest experience. Yet its existence can hardly be denied, and it is now no longer feasible to look for its causes in subjective faults, or in the interests of any particular group, such as bureaucracy or technocracy. Deeper, structural causes have intervened.

There is little data available to us about the growth in the power of management, if only because the analytical studies which deal with the way Yugoslav management works can to a large extent be characterised as apologias. However, the position is similar to what we may see in other European socialist countries, including Hungary of course, albeit in a different context and in defence of different social forms. But while we have few facts to substantiate the statement below, the force of logic as well as many individual experiences bear it out. Those opinions which deny that this is the situation, or that the trend toward bureaucratisation is prevalent, or those that ascribe it to subjective errors and at the most to the results of the particular interests of a social stratum, can very easily be shown to be full of misconceptions, frequently confusing what they feel ought to be with what actually exists:

"Instead of the expected redistribution of power, we have in most of the working organisations noted a reproduction of hierarchy in the system of self-management. Self-management has become something transmitted by the leading group in the enterprise, in other words, an auxiliary and complementary instrument in the hands of the leaders. Of course, self-management has considerably changed the status of the leading group in the enterprise.

"Usually the leading group retained all the power it had exercised previously, and delegated responsibility only for all those decisions and measures in which the organs of self-management became competent. So in many cases a completely unexpected process began, which could be called the 'illegalisation of management'. The self-managing organs accepted full responsibility for all essential decisions without having the appropriate specialised knowledge or the necessary social power to make this responsibility felt. Thus increasingly they became instead a front for the leading group which, taking cover behind the self-managing organs, were more or less managing the whole enterprise without being authorised. This is how the leading groups in the enterprises, intentionally or unintentionally, became cliques, keeping all the power in their own hands and yet not being responsible for their work."[14]

These statements do not detract from the historic merits of the Yugoslav communists who, by expounding the theory of "self-management" and building the institutions to practise "self-management", were the first to launch a general attack on the ideology of management monopoly, as the bearer of bureaucratic relations, which had developed in the socialist countries. However, we must repeatedly question whether, with the two different solutions in the socialist countries, the much-criticised and widely attacked bureaucracy is a series of subjective errors, and what it is that gives the bureaucracy of today its extraordinary strength and vitality.

Bearing this in mind, we must at the present stage of development in the socialist countries take into account the necessary and inevitable existence of separate administrations concerned with the tasks of management and direction, endowed with real power and with an extensive interest in their own activities—even if their existence brings about more than a few negative results and social anomalies, and essentially exhibits all the criteria which Marx regarded as the basic symptoms of the bureaucratic relation as a "substantial condition".

The third alternative: management power and social control

The historical experiences mentioned above are increasingly substantiating the need to work out and put into practice some new alternative, which will recognise that:

(a) *to some extent* management and direction provided by separate administrations in almost all social spheres is a speedier and more effective solution than management by laymen, and precisely for this reason will regard the building of management systems with their own interests, aims and power as unavoidable at society's present state of development; yet also

(b) *to some extent* it is necessary (since management systems inevitably develop special interests opposed to the interests of society as a whole) to make these management organs effectively dependent on society; or, in other words, to ensure the institutional *authority* of society over the *power* of management.

Marx regarded the ultimate aim to be a society without domination; but this can only be realised if and when power no longer exists. Until that situation comes about, social control as an institution is necessary. Real power today is centralised in the hands of the administration, and because of the lack of control over them a whole series of dangers and negative phenomena arise which can only be curbed or abolished through effective control by society. This problem is made all the more serious because as society evolves, there arise in quite varied walks of life management apparatuses (apart from the two alternatives referred to) which gain stability, which have a monopoly of administrative knowledge, and which in fact become more and more familiar with the "refined" social and psychological techniques for moulding people's behaviour.

In the Eastern European socialist countries a new situation has been created in the last decade, as a result of changes in both the internal and external power situations; and this favours the development of another alternative in which, with the growing efficiency of management, a movement to establish control over it by society is more and more likely to come about. The job of establishing the social dependence of, or control over, management

71

can no longer be overshadowed by the need to establish the new socialist power firmly (for it is now of course established in almost every respect), or by the basic aspects of economic reconstruction and development, for these are already in a position to ensure that all members of society are provided with the most important essentials of life.

In my opinion these two conditions are above all necessary if the creation of an institutional social authority over management power is to become the motivation and goal of a movement, and to be capable of being formulated as a realistic demand. Undoubtedly the practical development of this alternative will bring with it very substantial changes in the institutions which have developed up till now, as well as the formulation of a whole series of new institutions qualified to bring about in practice the control of management by society.

Foreseeably, as the changes occur, the present solution will have to be transcended in the following ways: assuring the hegemony of the direct producers and service workers; calling in experts, who are as independent of the administration as possible, to assist in society's controlling activities; creating a system of rotation which will make lobbying, at least on a mass scale, impossible in practice; developing the power of management along pluralist lines, creating counterpoints, in order to make it impossible for management power to act effectively as an integrated whole against its control by and dependence on society; and so on. By no means are we in a position today even to outline all these changes; for that, we need above all to recognise the basic problem itself and, on this basis, to initiate and develop a debate in which eventually even the details of the various concepts can be thrashed out.

This new alternative for the power structure of socialist society, like those before it, is very closely linked with the inevitable changes in the historical functions of the leninist communist workers' parties. Nothing is further from marxism than trying to turn the part played by the party into something above history and society.

In the struggle with reformist tendencies and also with revisionist social democratic parties, the leninist party emerged as the leading party in the workers' fight to achieve working-class dominance. The aim was to attain a position of dominance which could put an end to the right of private ownership of capital and to all those institutional forms of capitalist authority and power which were built on private ownership or intended for its protection at all costs. Without carefully weighing up this historic function of the leninist party, with all its consequences, it is not really possible to understand anything of the lessons to be learned from our recent history.

With the creation of working-class power, a new situation arose: when the party struggling for power became the party in power, again there were both positive and negative effects. (This new situation was particularly difficult for those parties which, through peculiarities of history, became organisations with a strong mass following only in this second phase.) Various possible ways of solving the new tasks appeared, but one thing was certain: in some form or other, a new type of state administrative system or civic discipline had to be constructed and stabilised. And this, as far as the subject we are discussing was concerned, meant that the most varied kinds of administration and managing institution had to be given real power.

Now, after the realisation of the conditions I referred to earlier, when there is really no longer any way by which the anti-progressive forces can make society revert to capitalist private ownership, and when through the development of economic strength the population's primary needs can be satisfied, a radically new situation is coming into being: the social conditions are being created for the leninist party to change from being the party in power to being the party fighting for society's control over the power of social administration.

To try to analyse the consequences of this change of function, and the movements which will evolve in the process, would take us too far in speculation. It is impossible to see today what the feasible outcome will be, if only because the European socialist countries are still very much at the start of this development that we have identified. Nevertheless, a consideration of events in Hungary in recent years will confirm the belief that the theoretical formulation of this possible alternative but also its practical realisation are realities of social history.

From this viewpoint, too, we regard as extremely significant the introduction of the new system of management, as well as the movement developing to assist it. This is still the case, even if we can only say at the moment that the new social aims and needs arising from the new situation are not yet clearly formulated but are simply evidence of *the pressure within the party for an analysis of the conditions which have developed, and of the resolute determination which is prepared for the most far-reaching changes in the interests of social progress.*

The concept of the new system of management goes far beyond

73

a simple intention to rationalise. The resolution on this topic proves that *the party is not inseparably bound either to management power* (by protecting the existing forms which have developed) or to tasks restricted to optimisation; if the development of social conditions demands this of it, *it is capable even of reforming itself.*

The three alternatives analysed briefly above were raised in the years immediately following the success of the socialist revolution, and were even formulated then, although not as an organised theory. The first alternative was worked out and supported by Trotsky, who was the protagonist of the creation of a monolithic state on a military model. (We should not be diverted by the fact that in the thirties Trotsky was the most violent critic of the solution which he himself had been the first to formulate in theory, but which was actually put into practice under Stalin's leadership.) The second alternative was supported by the representatives of the "Workers' Opposition". They wanted the workers, or rather the trade unions as the workers' representatives, to elect the economic leaders at the most varied level of economic administration, from foreman to people's commissar. They stood for the committee method, for "collective leadership" rather than leadership by responsible individuals. When they demanded trade union rights, they did not discern the essential distinction (formulated by the Webbs nearly two decades previously) between management by the trade unions—bureaucratic direction— on the one hand, and management by the direct producers on the other.

When I come to look for the origins of the third alternative, I find myself in a very difficult position. To some extent it seems to me to be unequivocally demonstrable that Lenin perceived, even if he did not formulate it in such a way, the difference between management power and the authority of society. On the other hand, however, I am far from convinced that Lenin saw everything correctly, or that what Lenin thought of any one view is conclusive evidence of its correctness.

Yet Lenin did recognise two important things, although he was not to find time to work out in detail the theory of the socialist state. The first was that in the socialist state there would necessarily and inevitably evolve management systems in which bureaucratic conditions (in the marxist sense) would again be created; secondly, that the socialist society would have to do everything possible to bring about control of these systems by the ordinary workers (meaning essentially those doing direct manual labour). He was a long way from stating that this controlling function

74

would be the privilege of *individuals;* he wanted *the whole of society* to participate in the control of management, to teach *everyone* how to perform this function.

Of course, Lenin was well aware that if socialist power, this "child Hercules", was to survive, it could not rely on the traditional democratic "rights to freedom". Yet he did not make a generalisation out of the temporary need for the limitation of democratic rights.

This retrospective glance into history is not meant to be proof of anything, unless it is that in the early twenties, the leninist period which we continually refer to, it was possible to consider the alternatives for socialist development, and that in the half-century that has passed since then one of the greatest achievements has been that *once again* not only is it a possibility for us, but also a necessity and a duty.

VI: The Relevance of the "Trade Union Debate"

In approaching the current problems of socialist development we can seek valuable guidance not only in the classical works of marxism, but also in the discussions and experiences of the decade following the October revolution. This is why it is worthwhile analysing this period, in which the options for socialist development had already been formulated in the practice of socialist construction, but in which socialist thinking had not yet been shut within the confines of a particular solution. As as result of this realisation it has currently become "fashionable" to rediscover the significance of the political arguments and theoretical debates of the decade following the October revolution and free them from the dogmatic interpretation predominant during the Stalin period.

One of the most relevant episodes in this phase of development is the so-called "trade union debate" which took place in the Soviet Union between 1920 and 1922, that is to say over a relatively short period of time. In this essay I shall treat the "trade union debate" not from the standpoint of the historian, but from the perspective of whether it contributes to the solution of our contemporary theoretical and practical problems, and if so, how. Can the questions formulated in this debate still be instructive for us after nearly half a century, and if they are, then to what extent?

The introduction of the Hungarian economic reform, which is still in its initial phase, increasingly compels us to consider the functions of our most important socio-political organisations and institutions. This task is more and more frequently tackled in our periodicals, if only in the form of first attempts at formulation. If, in my investigation of the relevance of the "trade union debate" of the 1920s, I consider the problem of the trade unions in isolation from the complex of the extraordinarily closely-knit questions surrounding it, I by no means wish to imply that this nexus of problems can be treated as an autonomous phenomenon independent of socio-political reforms; I am nevertheless of the opinion that analysis of this sector can further the clarification and analysis of the path of social development which we consider correct.

76

The "statification" of the trade union and the "syndicalisation" of the state as a unity in practice

The relationship between the new type of socialist state and the trade union was at the centre of the debate in the Soviet Union. This is a problem without any historical precedent, an entirely new situation in which a series of difficult questions was posed. After a while, this principal question was formulated as an unavoidable either/or choice — *either* state direction of the economy must be made the business of the trade unions ("syndicalisation of the state"), *or* the trade unions must dissolve into the existing organs of state ("statification" of the trade unions). Immediately after the revolution these two possibilities, held strictly separate in the later course of the debate, still continued to constitute a unity both in theory and practice, and were not yet divided into two conflicting conceptions. As late as 1919 Lenin expressed himself as follows, at the second Trade Union Congress: "The transformation of trade unions into organs of the state has become unavoidable, it has become unavoidable for them to fuse with the organs of state power, it has become unavoidable that the development of large-scale production be put entirely in their hands." Thus theory could not yet perceive any contradiction between the "statification" of the trade unions and the "syndicalisation" of the state. In order for what follows to be better understood, however, I must add two comments to this point: the objective cited above did not seem immediately realisable to Lenin, and thus presented itself not as a tactical proposition, but as a strategic aim which, while the first term must admittedly be subordinated to it, could only be the result of a lengthy period of historical development; furthermore, Lenin considered the statification of the trade unions to be a process identical with the graduation of working people to the running of the state, a process in which the first term was to be grasped as an external form of development and the second as its content. To understand Lenin's posing of the problem we must also take into account the historical situation itself, the practice within which the new state administrative apparatus began to be elaborated and with it the divergent development of state and trade unions.

"State organisation of industry", wrote Kritsman, one of the participants in the trade union discussion, "entirely corresponded to the structure of the trade unions, with the exception of small-scale industry, which was of merely local significance: it was undertaken in terms of the particular branches of industry," so

77

that economic organs were built up "directly upon the organisations of the proletariat".[15] For this reason alone, it was entirely natural that collective leadership, or "the collegiate principle" as it was known at the time, was initially retained and was similarly predominant in the management of the economy.

The construction of a separate state apparatus nevertheless took greater and greater precedence, and the separation of the state and trade unions became increasingly distinct. All this tied in closely with the efforts to consolidate the Soviet state and the conditions under which the creation of the state apparatus proceeded. The proposed resolution on the tasks of the trade unions prepared for the first Trade Union Congress by the communist faction already states: "The trade unions must, during the period of the dictatorship of the workers and peasants, be organs of the socialist state, as such working together with the other organs towards the realisation of the new organisational foundations of the economy and society."[16] (The same draft resolution also envisaged compulsory membership of trade unions. At the time, however, this manner of posing the question raised doubts even in the communist faction, which incidentally represented two-thirds of the members of the congress; thus, the party did not in fact reject the problem of statification, but it did not seem an immediate issue to them. The either/or choice was already beginning to crystallise, however.)

The contradiction becomes acute

Towards the end of 1919 and the beginning of 1920 we encounter increasingly distinct signs of the process whereby the state apparatus and the trade unions became separate from each other, not only in practice, but also in the sphere of ideology. While on the one hand the bureaucratic conception of administration later known as "glavkism" was developing, anarcho-syndicalist perspectives gripped the trade unions on the other (1920 saw a new upswing of anarchism in Soviet political and intellectual life).

In this situation the relationship between state and trade union also took on a new light. The formerly unitary conception was advanced as two opposing theses: (a) the trade unions must be taken under state control on the grounds that the state is the organisation of the revolutionary working class, beside which any external interest must be counter-revolutionary or at the very least conservative; (b) the state must be subordinate to the direct control of the trade unions since even the Soviet state is, like any other, an administrative apparatus separate from the immediate producers, "a bureaucratic outgrowth", an abcess on the body of society. The staunchest advocate of the former conception was Trotsky, of the second the "Workers' Opposition" (Shlyapnikov).

What is interesting is the fact that nobody questioned the inevitability of state and trade union fusing. Milyutin, for example, states in the argument with Trotsky: "Nobody would deny the inevitability of the state economic apparatus and the trade unions fusing, the issue is rather at what pace and in what form the process of fusing should proceed."[17] Whereas the two sharply opposed factions both saw this as the general objective, there were also important differences between them over (a) their assessment of the situation in the trade unions, (b) their view of the essential functions of the trade unions and (c) following on from these two points, what method they considered appropriate for uniting state and trade union.

In order to understand what followed, it is of prime importance to look into the origins of the alternative advocated by Trotsky. Trotsky proceeded upon the view that after the revolution the trade unions were in a state of crisis which should be seen not, as some maintained, as growing pains, but as a "death-agony". A similar point of view also gave rise to suggestions that the trade unions should be dissolved and their functions allocated to other suitable organs. We must note in this context that Trotsky was by no means the most radical in his conclusions on this point. He proceeded upon the assumption that state and trade union had no divergent functions; so that in the case of the metal-workers' union and the administration of the metallurgical industry, for example, both had to fulfil the same tasks and for this purpose appoint the same specialists. From here it was but a step to formulating the idea of making the trade union part of the state.

Despite his definite, principled position, Trotsky did not propose any precise programme. He emphasised that it was not the formal "statification" of the trade unions that mattered, demanding rather that trade unions become state organs of production in practice, embracing the whole of industry and bearing responsibility both for production and producers. This was also emphasised in Trotsky's and Bukharin's common programme. As early as the Ninth Congress of the CPSU, Trotsky brought the need to militarise industry into the debate and severely criticised Smirnov who, in an article published in *Pravda*, had expressed doubts on this in referring to the role of the trade unions. He underlined the importance of a unified national economic plan and censured the Supreme National Economic Council of the Union for their previous neglect of this question. Finally, concerning the question of one-man management, he stressed that executive posts must be filled solely with regard to technical expertise. On 21 July 1920 he made a speech to the second All-Russian Congress of Railway Unions in which he unambiguously asserted that the sole significance of trade unions lay in advancing production. His standpoint was thus, as we have seen, consistently centred on the state, so that the continued existence of trade unions as a movement could only be disturbing for him.

While Trotsky wanted to make trade unions part of the state, Shlyapnikov and what was called the "Workers' Opposition" wanted, in Trotsky's phrase, to "syndicalise" the state. The Workers' Opposition was able to base itself on the party programme, which stated unambiguously that the administration of industry must be put into the hands of the trade unions at every level. The relevant sentence, frequently cited in the debate, runs: "The trade unions must come to concentrate the entire management of the whole national economy in their hands as a unified economic whole." The Workers' Opposition interpreted this programme as a tactical objective to be put into practice immediately, and not as a strategic one. Lozovsky's criticism was also primarily directed against the Workers' Opposition's disregard of the concrete conditions of 1920, but he himself stuck unambiguously to this point in the programme as a strategic demand.

Shlyapnikov directly counterposed the trade unions to the Soviet organs of state, seeing the latter as bureaucratic machinery by their very nature. Thus he writes: "The devastation can only be overcome and the productive forces of our country only recreated and increased if the system now in existence, the practical methods of organising and administering the national economy, are fundamentally changed. The system and method of construction resting on a ponderous bureaucratic apparatus rule out any creative initiative, every independent act on the part of the producers organised in the trade unions."[18]

French syndicalism undoubtedly exercised an influence on the trade union opposition, at least as regards the former's principles on the future organisation of society. This influence was strengthened by the fact that, like Russian communism, albeit under different concrete historical conditions, French syndicalism arose in opposition to social democratic parties which had declined into the opportunism of parliamentary and electoral campaigns and been integrated into capitalist society. Sorel, however, unlike Lenin,

80

did not advocate a revolution of the poor, but revolutionary uprising in a situation in which capitalism was in full development. This is a major reason why anarcho-syndicalist efforts failed in the Soviet Union, for what occurred was a revolution of the poor in which, after the devastation of the world war and the civil war, the development of production and the abolition of hunger were put uppermost; in the prevailing historical situation this imperatively demanded centralism and the introduction of discipline and forced labour in the strict sense of the term.

In the view of anarcho-syndicalism the ideal society of the future was a society oriented towards the self-administration of freely associated working people; the negation of the state in this movement, which called itself neo-marxist in its ideology, has its intellectual roots in anarchism. The "most simply organised" system was to be based on the statistical assessment of needs and productive capacities. Each profession was to be organised into a syndicate, each syndicate would elect a council, the professional labour council; these syndicates would associate into federations on the national and international scale according to their branch of production. It is not hard to see the kinship between the trade union-centred perspectives of the Workers' Opposition and the standpoint of anarcho-syndicalism, according to which the society of the future would be based entirely on the trade unions or "free associations of producers". (The difference and lack of correspondence between trade union and "free association of producers" could not be recognised in the prevailing historical situation.) It is much harder to demonstrate the influence of anarchism in Russia on the programme of the trade union opposition, although this was no doubt also significant. This current must at any rate be taken into consideration in order to understand the divergent viewpoint that arose within the communist movement and marxism. Particularly in 1918 and 1920, the anarchist tendencies grew in the Soviet Union. The debates which developed between anarchists and communists no longer referred to the state in general, but specifically to the state of the dictatorship of the proletariat, or in other words the organised power of workers and peasants.

There can be little doubt that in historical terms the anarchists played a significant role in the victory of the October revolution. According to Preobrazhensky's analysis, three currents developed among them after the revolution: (a) some, a minority, supported the struggle of the power of the soviets against the national and international bourgeoisie; (b) a fraction relatively small in numerical terms recognised that the Soviet state differed from previous states, but nevertheless considered itself bound to wage struggle against it; (c) the third group, the majority, made a distinction between the Soviet state, which they fought, and the soviets, which they supported. They considered them to be not organs of "power", but organs of the will of the "working population".[19]

In a resolution taken at the Elisabetengrad Congress, the anarchists stated: "Under the concrete conditions in Russia the direct transition from big-bourgeois tsarism to anarchist society can be realised immediately; the main obstacle to this is the state communists, who are attempting to organise the proletariat into a state class and who, in contradiction to the interests of the workers, do not want the immediate liquidation of Soviet power and direct transition to a non-authoritarian society." The well-known slogan of the anarchists, "No compromise with Soviet power!", derives from this. As a movement, anarchism in Russia came into direct confrontation with communism and, from that point on, anarchism and hostility to the Soviet Union became identical terms.

Lenin's attempt to eliminate the conflict between theory and practice

Basing themselves primarily on the trade unions' growing membership, Lenin, Zinoviev and others denied the existence of a crisis, and even went so far as to perceive definite progress, though at the same time having no illusions about the continuing weakness of the trade unions in relation to what was being demanded of them.

A factor characteristic of the situation, although not decisive, is revealed when the membership of the trade unions and that of the party are compared:

YEAR	Membership of UNIONS and PARTY in Russia	
1917	693,000	23,600
1918	1,946,000	115,000
1919	3,707,000	251,000
1920	5,222,000	431,400

The fact that membership was growing does not by itself rule out crisis, the cause of which is primarily to be sought in the increasing conflicts between the movement aspects and the organisation aspects, between the functions of administering the economy and defending the interests of the members. It must also be remembered that the role of the unions in the administration of the economy

changed considerably from the end of 1921 on, a change characterised as follows by Lozovsky: "The Supreme Economic Council
is being reorganised on a new basis. Its departments no longer
consist as formerly of a majority of trade union representatives,
the unions no longer control the work of the organs of the
economy, but rather give their attention to labour questions,
supporting the work of the state organs in the improvement of
production by their experience." The Supreme National Economic
Council and the central leadership of the Soviet trade unions were
working in parallel, yet independently of each other. This state of
affairs, as the quotation above shows, was not ideal in Lozovsky's
view, and at the end of his article he writes: "Every step forward
in the revolution means a step forward for the unions towards
the appropriation of production. The definitive transfer of the productive apparatus of the whole country into the hands of the
unions will take place with the final victory of the world revolution."[20]

After a short period practice showed that a separate administrative machinery had developed, fundamentally different in its
guiding principles both from that of the unions and that of the
party organisations; and if we are to look for analogies, it rather
resembled the organisation of an army (and, not by chance, it
was Trotsky, the supreme commander of the Red Army, who
most clearly formulated this analogy) or the organisational forms
of high-concentration capitalism (a recognition which contributed
to the tempestuous growth in popularity of taylorism in the Soviet
Union in the early 1920s) as socio-political movements. Practice
contradicted the principles by which marxists had earlier oriented
themselves towards post-revolutionary administrative activity. Confrontation between principles and the actual situation became
unavoidable.

The most important issue was the attitude to be taken towards
the bureaucratic character of the Soviet state as it was now constituted. Nobody denied the danger of bureaucracy, but the
opinions which were held about its cause and character became
all the more divergent. Bukharin, who made common cause with
Trotsky in the trade union debate, also recognised the fact of
"bureaucratic distortion" and wrote: "We cannot deny that, as
a whole and as a set of subordinate organs, our state apparatus
at present suffers from bureaucratic deformation and will continue
to do so for some time."[21] In this we can see two important theses
operating: bureaucratic development is a disease (which can of
course also have subjective causes), but it is a persistent one.

According to Trotsky, no external—that is, social—forces are needed to correct bureaucracy, and the state apparatus is capable of correcting itself. This is something which Lenin was doubtful of, and in the course of the trade union debate he stated in opposition to Trotsky's position that, at a time "when bureaucracy confronts the masses in transparent form", the struggle against bureaucracy could not be waged solely through the state's efforts at self-correction, but also needed an external force, the organisations of the working population. These fought bureaucracy by the very fact of defending the interests of their members.

Unlike Trotsky, Lenin, who had called for the rapid incorporation of the trade unions into the state after the October revolution, had by the beginning of 1920 come to the view that great caution had been shown to be necessary on this question. According to Lozovsky, Lenin already foresaw the first signs of the NEP, and also clearly sensed the unions' problem to be that they had stopped being trade unions when they had taken over the whole burden and responsibility of economic management, so that the workers had no alternative but to found new unions. Towards the end of 1920 it became apparent to him "that we are faced here with a complex system involving many cogs, not a simple system by any means",[22] and that because of this it was necessary to find the right division of labour between economic organisations and trade unions.

Besides this, it remained a political priority of the first order to secure communist influence. Only two years previously the mensheviks had raised the demand for independent trade unions under menshevik leadership to defend the interests of the working class against the state. As far as many people were concerned, they compromised the slogan of defence of workers' interests irretrievably in doing so; this must also be taken into consideration when we look at Lenin's cautious-seeming formulations.

Nevertheless, the platform elaborated by Lenin, Zinoviev and others quite unambiguously stressed, in opposition to Trotsky's conception, that "it is necessary for the trade unions to remain schools of communism, organisers of the masses, and on no account to become organs of the state in too narrow a sense."[23] "Workers of different views and attitudes, party members and non-members, the literate and the illiterate, believers and atheists, and so on" should all belong to the trade unions. The platform does recognise that the unions are having to take on more and more state functions; but, in the opinion of the authors, that is no reason why they should abandon the form of mass organisation. It is not difficult to show that this position was attempting to integrate the most extremely opposed views. The functions of the unions are systematised on this basis, as follows: (1) the formation of economic organs; (2) participation in working out economic plans and programmes; (3) the supervisory function; (4) the distribution of labour resources around the different sectors of production (labour resource policy, as we should say today); (5) wages policy (the platform wanted to transfer this completely to the unions); (6) working out the production programme (also entirely the task of the unions according to the platform); (7) preserving work discipline and disciplinary arrangements.

Integral to Lenin's plan, which demanded both the development of a sophisticated administrative apparatus and genuine social control over it, was the notion of inspection by workers and peasants, the intention being to put this social control on a broader basis than the trade unions, on the worker and peasant masses; this seemed to diminish the danger of bureaucratic machinery having the right of regulation rather than the masses. Lenin had no illusions over the fact that up to 1920 inspection by workers and peasants represented a desideratum rather than a reality, since the best of the working class were at the front and the peasants' cultural level was very modest; precisely because of this, he energetically began to work out the theoretical foundations of a new institutional form of social control. Proceeding upon a resolution taken in 1919 itself, "state inspection" was in 1920 changed into "inspection by workers and peasants" with the aim of "carrying out supervision of the state administration, of every organ of the economic and social institutions, with participation by the broad masses of the workers".[24] Members of the inspecting body were elected by those working in the factories, larger institutions and villages and charged with informing their constituents regularly about their activity. From the start there was great opposition to this new form of inspection; *Ekonomicheskaya zhizn'*, for example, devoted two articles to a polemic against "the principle of prior control" and demanded a documented, specialist inspection operating retrospectively.

A crucial question in the development of inspection was whether professional and inevitably bureaucratic inspection could be reconciled with the genuine participation of the working masses of the kind both Lenin and the official "Inspectorate" organ insisted upon, with every worker gradually taking part in inspection work and thus getting to know in practice the problems of managing society. (The "Workers' and Peasants' Inspectorate" did not confine itself to economic life and state administration in a narrow sense: thus we read in its official organ for 1920 that the work of the Moscow crime police has been examined. This article clearly confirms the humanistic conception of the "inspectors"; the suggestions put forward deal specifically with the improvement of conditions in the prisons.[25])

The ending of the "trade union debate"

1920 was the year of great triumph for the Soviet system, and it is not by chance that at this point it became possible to discuss the various options for development. The maturity and high level of these discussions give glowing testimony to the extraordinary intellectual power at the disposal of the Soviet revolution.

The phase of open debate did not last long, however; the Kronstadt uprising and the famine caused by the bad harvest of 1921 opened a new period in which unbroken unity unambiguously became the foremost principle once again. In the Volga region the grain harvest came to 98.4m. pud when at least 264.4m. were needed. "The famine in the Volga region is increasing in severity. Thirteen million people, a tenth of the inhabitants of the republic, are starving."[26] This made it easier for one particular perspective of development to become dominant.

The thinking of the Workers' Opposition was condemned to failure for many reasons in this concrete historical situation. The difficult economic and political situation demanded reinforcement of the state apparatus, almost at any price—not merely primary capital accumulation, but poverty and hunger also made it necessary; the transfer of the management of the economy to the trade unions would have directly threatened the political hegemony so recently secured. Precisely because of this, the tenth Congress of the CPSU emphatically stated that the trade unions "must gradually be turned into organs supplementing the proletarian state, and not the reverse". The rejection of the Workers' Opposition platform, however, by no means signified the victory of Trotsky's views. The trade union debate came to a close in the atmosphere of NEP, a situation of extreme economic and political tension, with the resolution of the party's central committee which stated Lenin's lines of thinking as follows: "The trade unions must take it upon themselves to defend the interests of the workers, to further the raising of their material standard of living so far as is possible, constantly correcting the errors and excesses of the economic organs resulting from bureaucratic deformation of the state apparatus." The resolution deduces from this the contradictory character of trade union work, and certain passages are worth quoting in greater detail: "On the one hand, persuasion and education are the most important elements in their method of working; on the other hand, they do not even themselves deny that they participate in the exercise of state power and coercion. On the one hand, their main function lies in the defence of the interests of the working masses in the most direct and narrow sense of the word, on the other hand we cannot deny that they take part in oppression by participating in the exercise of state power and constructing the entire national economy. . . . These contradictions are not accidental and can only be abolished in several decades' time."[27]

At the same time as the 1921 resolution, the main emphasis changed, for practical reasons, from the argument against Trotsky's position to struggle against the Workers' Opposition. There was a campaign for the reduction of the trade union machinery which did not, however, in any way affect the nature of trade union management. Tomsky, for example, recommended that the European unions and the German ones in particular should be taken as an example of rationalisation, although it was already well-known that they had built up a strong bureaucracy on a broad base.

The debate was thus resolved, but the resolution of the Tenth Party Congress attacked the formation of factions and, taking the situation of the country into consideration, advocated continued discussion together with "the absolutely necessary criticism of the errors of the party, analysis of the general line of the party.". It simultaneously took measures to ensure that the entire party membership was acquainted with these discussions; the regular appearance of a "discussion paper" was to further this end.

It is equally characteristic of the conditions thus arising that the resolution of the Tenth Party Congress "On the unity of the party and the prohibition of the formation of factions in the party" continues to refer to "the struggle against bureaucracy and the extension of democracy" in conjunction with one another. Preobrazhensky wrote in publicising this resolution, "the struggle against anarchist and social revolutionary attitudes in particular strata of the proletariat must not inhibit the fight against bureaucracy and the failings of the Soviet apparatus, but rather reinforce it".[28]

Lozovsky's prophecy cited above, about the trade unions gradually extending their power, was not fulfilled. He himself, a faithful leninist who for a long time led the international trade union movement, fell victim to the caprices of the "personality cult". The trade union movement itself, however, was sacrificed in this period; what Trotsky had most openly advocated in the trade union debate came to pass—the trade unions fused with the organs of state, in real, if not in formal terms.

The principal function of the trade unions became to bring about the realisation of state plans. Work competition, managed from above and largely manipulated, became their principal contribution to the fulfilment of production plans; their management of this competition, together with the support they gave to the fixing of norms, alienated the working masses from the trade unions and, it may be said, robbed the latter completely of their character as a movement. At the same time, the trade unions' function of being, as Lenin put it, the schools of communism became a formality. Two factors simultaneously stood in the way of this being successful: it was not possible to articulate the views of various groups of the working class within the trade unions, so that the victory of communist ideas in debate was not possible; and the trade unions' function of choosing and training workers for the administrative machinery also gradually disappeared.

In compensation, as it were, the socialist state transferred far-reaching administrative powers to the unions, but these merely intensified their role in the state apparatus, for by themselves they made the development of a powerful administrative apparatus necessary. Not only did the unions become organs of the state (albeit not in a formal sense), but the character of the workers' and peasants' inspection also changed: this institution, which according to Lenin's plan was to introduce the working masses to the control of society, was transformed into a bureaucratic apparatus of control as the result of a series of reorganisations. As early as the Seventeenth Party Congress, Stalin sanctioned this development: "We now need an organisation which, while not taking upon itself the universal goal of inspecting each and every factor, would be capable of giving its entire attention to checking that the decisions of the central institutions of the Soviet state are carried out. An organisation of this kind can only be a commission for Soviet supervision attached to the Council of Peoples' Commissars of the Soviet Union, working on the basis of the

Councils' instructions and having representatives independent of the local organs in the individual localities."[29] Thus, according to Stalin's formulation, the local organs were to be excluded from the exercise of inspection, as well as the masses.

Although no debate on trade unions arose during these years—practice and principles had apparently attained eternal unity—the problem of ordering society democratically and that of the trade union movement posed themselves more and more acutely in reality. Already by the time of the Twentieth Congress of the CPSU many signs in the socialist countries of Europe pointed to a developing process of criticism of that practice, the most tragic effects of which were seen in our own country.

The trade unions and the New Economic Reform

After 1956 many of the mistakes originating in earlier practice were corrected in our country in the reorganised trade union movement (abolition of the formal characteristics of labour competition, of the extremely negative role of the trade unions in the fixing of norms, etc.). But it was only with the transition to the economic reform that examination and revision of the functions of the trade unions which went back to their historical origins and genuinely confronted reality with principles became possible and necessary. The economic reform gave the trade union debate a new relevance, for the structure of power in economic life has been undergoing an extremely significant modification involving the function of the trade unions in an entirely new fashion. Certain aspects of this now ineluctable problematic have already been formulated, although at present we still have far to go not only for divergent views to be integrated, but even for the various positions to crystallise.

Previous experience of the construction of socialism shows that the dichotomy "syndicalisation of the state" versus "statification of the unions" is no longer relevant. Socialist society is developing in a pluralist direction, and the functions of the state administration and those of the unions are becoming increasingly independent of one another. In comparison with the Stalin era, the trade unions are increasingly taking on the new task of defending the interests of the workers and exercising social control over the administration.

Let us first consider the trade unions as organs for the defence of the workers' interests. The problems most interesting in this connection were broached in our country by the debate between

89

Rezso Nyers (one of the initiators of the economic reform) and Gabor Somoskoi (a leading trade union official). We will begin with the interpretation of the past. During the Stalin era, the function of defending the workers' interests faded out completely. It might be thought superfluous to point this fact out in our country today; but Gabor Somoskoi writes: "The defence of legitimate individual interests has been in the past and remains today the primary objective of wage- and salary-earners in founding and supporting a trade union." What is the origin of this misconception? It can hardly be denied that this statement fails to make any distinction between the declared and actual function of the trade union. It is true that our unions have never renounced the defence of the workers' interests, but for many years they did not exercise this function. They held the declared, general interests of society and that of the working class to be identical, and thus took the view that their participation in the fixing of norms and the abolition of "free movement of labour" was in the interest of the working class. We have left this level of argument far behind, a proposition expressed by Rezso Nyers when he says: "The unions are primarily organs for the defence of the interests of workers engaged in different trades. I would not say that they are organs defending the interests of the 'working population'. It is only in a very mediated way and through various intermediaries that the 'working population' expresses itself as a constituency of interests in the unions. It is the specific trade, the specific worker, the specific white-collar worker, each with their own interests, that are dominant in the unions. Of course, this also amounts to a general economic interest of workers and white-collar workers, in so far as professional interests can be reduced to a common denominator."[30]

The demand for unions to represent the *general* interest of the working class is dangerous, since it can easily mean a return to the formula of the past by which we took the general interest of society, the interests of the working class and the interests of the unions to be absolutely identical.

All these considerations are not intended to rule out the possibility of the trade union apparatus or the trade union movement being able to express the integrated interest of the working class—nor does Comrade Nyers intend to say this; but this would mean advocating a trade union movement within which the interests of the different professions can be integrated, not merely the acceptance of declared goals. Social and historical experience shows that the unions are in a position to practise the defence of workers'

90

interests, primarily in the sense that they represent the interests of the individual workforces of each factory, professional groups and individual employees, although, as the experiences of the debate discussed above confirm, a real assessment of the past is involved in the correct interpretation even of this function.

The problem poses itself very differently in respect of social control. Here, the central problem without doubt consists in the realisation of the workforce's rights to exercise real supervision over the factory management, which implies the demand that factory managements should be dependent for their existence upon the workforce, the members of which in turn are in the power of and personally dependent for their existence upon management, at least as far as their specific jobs are concerned. As an integral component of the realisation of social control over management this is an entirely new function, the forms of which could not develop in the capitalist countries, and which must therefore be developed within socialism as something entirely novel, without any precedent.

In this essay I have attempted to demonstrate that this notion arose in the early 1920s in the conception of the tasks of the unions, particularly in the ideal of a workers' and peasants' inspection scheme in which each working person would at some point serve and thus learn the techniques of administration.

During the elaboration of the economic reform, the attempt was made in our country to make this idea a reality through the institution of the so-called "supervisory committees", which meant basically that committees elected by workers were to be formed at the various levels of management, committees in which the principle that no incumbent could hold more than one office was strictly upheld (managers and members of the administrative apparatus could not be elected) and which were complemented by specialists also independent of the administrative apparatus. According to this conception. the supervisory committee would in the main be dependent on movements, on the public, on the public sentiments of factory workforces and "the rest of society". They would have no particular area of authority, no permanent personnel, their activity would not be laid down by precise regulations, they would remain a movement seeking to realise the hegemony of society over the power of the administration.

As soon as this plan was first formulated, determined resistance to the realisation of this conception appeared from two quarters: (a) the managers of the state enterprises did not want to exchange their responsibility towards ministries for a social responsibility—

to exchange a familiar responsibility for an unfamiliar one; (b) on the other hand, the unions saw in the supervisory committees a competing influence and feared for the integrity of their preserve. The resistance under the first heading can be seen as a natural phenomenon as it were, but the second kind of resistance is intimately bound up with the basic concern of this essay, the "trade union debate".

Thorough study of past experience shows that only trade unions which, in addition to defending the material interests of working people, take upon themselves the struggle to realise the hegemony of society over the administration and put this objective before the narrower definition of their aims can contribute to socialist development.

The "trade union debate" is thus entering into a new and more advanced phase. The tasks which have meanwhile grown in importance and which pose themselves differently from before—the functions of representing the workers' interests and of social control—cannot be carried out by the state administration or even by the now bureaucratic trade union apparatus; only the real movement of the working people, or rather, their movements, is capable of fulfilling these functions. But very much depends upon whether the workers can depend on support from unions which have overcome their own individual and narrowly conceived interests, or whether they are embarking on a path of development sown with obstacles, certainly time-consuming and in opposition to the unions —perhaps thus risking a false polarisation.

VII: Towards a Sociological Analysis of Property* Relations

"There is a continual movement of growth in productive forces, of destruction in social relations, of formation in ideas; the only immutable thing is the abstraction of movement—*mors immortalis.*"

Marx, *The Poverty of Philosophy.*

One of the most characteristic features of the marxist theory of society has been to prove the outstanding importance of the dominant property relations in the life of concrete social and economic formations, and to deduce from these essential relations the existence of historical forces such as classes and class struggles. Marx explained how differing socio-economic formations develop and succeed each other primarily through the changes in property relations which result from these social struggles, and from the development of the forces of production; and he defined the periods of social progress mainly on the basis of the changes that occur in this respect. Therefore, if we wish to analyse the socialist societies of our time on a marxist basis, our main point of departure must be the property relations which have developed in them. And first of all we have to ask whether the problem of property (in the marxist sense) exists in these countries as a vital existential problem for a particular class or stratum, just as the abolition of feudal property relations was an existential problem for the bourgeois classes, or just as in nineteenth-century Europe it was the fundamental interest of the working class to transform bourgeois property relations.

It is especially difficult to examine questions of this kind in the social sciences, because every conclusion which the researcher reaches on the basis of his examination of the facts may collide with certain ideological tenets and even with political interests. But they are the problems which most demand a scientific analysis of social relations, in the interests of both practice and the progress

---

* Throughout this essay the words "property" and "ownership", "proprietor" and "owner" are synonymous, whereas "possession" is one of the *functions* of "ownership".

of scientific thought; and they demand that we go beyond the unquestioning adoption of positions.

Property relations as the "organising principle" of social relations

According to Marx, property relations are always embedded in society as a whole; that is to say, they do not consist solely in the ownership of objects, but are a kind of central point in the complex system of relationships between different classes and strata. Marx demonstrated that ownership of the means of production is the essential social relationship upon which all the complex inter-relations among people are built. As early as *Moralising Critique and Critical Morals*, he wrote that bourgeois private property was "the sum total of the bourgeois relations of production". In Oskar Lange's words, this meant that "the ownership of the means of production . . . is the foundation, or we might say the 'organising principle' which determines both the relations of production and the relations of distribution."[31] In Marx's approach, the notion of property relations as essential social relations is one of the points of departure for any deep-going social analysis; it must be understood that they are embedded in social relations (mainly productive ones) as a whole. Marx wrote in *The Poverty of Philosophy*: "To define bourgeois property thus is simply to give an exposition of all the social relations of bourgeois production. To try to give a definition of property as an independent relation, a category apart, an abstract and eternal idea, can be nothing but an illusion of metaphysics or of jurisprudence."

This quotation gives rise to two seemingly topical questions. How can one describe socialist property, in socialism, without taking into account all the essential social relations which are dominant in these societies? Why should the attempt to do so be anything but "an illusion of metaphysics and jurisprudence"?

If we want to know what are the essential social relations of socialist property relations, and whether a basic property problem exists in the socialist countries, then we must first survey all those social consequences in which these property relations are mani-fested, and in which they assume a concrete form. What I am therefore seeking are the phenomena through which property relations as essential social relations "materialise" into decisions and social action, in the same way that the immanent, essential attribute of the commodity, its value, expresses itself in the price. I term the exercise of property relations in this sense "ownership-exercise"*, and I include the following legal and practical capacities within the scope of this concept; (a) the capacity to direct people's activities as the executors of productive labour, i.e. the exercise of *power* and the directing of people; (b) the capacity for disposition over the means of production and the structure of production, i.e. the directing of objects; (c) the capacity to use, appropriate or at least distribute the surplus product; (d) the capacity to alienate and transfer by hereditary means the objects of property, the means of production or financial capital. And if it is not the owner in the juridical sense who practises these capacities, then the question of control over the practice of these rights arises.

In the course of history these capacities to decide and to act, which can be included in the concept of "ownership-exercise", have not always belonged to the *juridical* owner; either through some legal provision or simply through social custom, the owner may not in fact practise some of the capacities which come under the concept of ownership-exercise—he may have assigned them to others, or they may have been assigned to others compulsorily by society. In various ways, and to a greater or lesser extent, a type of restricted ownership-exercise has arisen, separate from the juridical owner, mainly in respect of capacities (a), (b) and (c), though not of (d). I shall call this restricted type of ownership-exercise "possession" or "possessing", in accordance with Marx's terminology.

The essential difference between property and possession is often obliterated, both in everyday parlance and in scientific thinking. Marx spoke about the serf under feudalism being a direct producer who was not a proprietor but only a possessor, and whose surplus labour belonged to the land owner. But Oskar Lange, for example, took property to be a type of possession which is socially recognised and protected, and in fact he put the emphasis on possession:

"The fundamental relationship among men is brought about on the basis of possession of the means of production. What we are dealing with here is not chance possession, but possession recognised by the members of society, which is guarded by the socially recognised rules of human coexistence and perhaps by the sanctions meted out against the contravention of

---

* This term translates a neologism in the Hungarian, *tulojdonlás*. It must be read throughout this essay in the light of Hegedus's definition here.

95

these rules, i.e. by custom and by law. This kind of possession is called property."[32]

But in history, property on the one hand, and possession as restricted ownership-exercise on the other, have often been separated in the way that I have explained. I therefore consider it justified to consider possession to be the manifestation of property relations as an essential relation, in which various forms and degrees of separation from the juridical proprietor may develop.

Unless we are to remain content with the abstractions of jurisprudence or ideology, we must first of all survey those consequences of socialist property relations which manifest themselves in ownership-exercise or possession. The analysis of these consequences is the most important aspect of the sociological examination of property relations, although it must be remembered that just as the price of goods is not exactly identical with their value, ownership-exercise and possession are also mere expressions of property relations as the essential relations of the whole society.

Property and Power

When the notions of property and power are placed alongside each other, they revive debates which are centuries old. Without trying to give any exact definition, I mean by "power" the legal and practical capacity, supplied by the division of labour, of individual persons or groups to influence the behaviour of other persons with consequences for the latter's livelihood, and to determine their own behaviour themselves. Thus essentially, though with some amplification, I adopt Max Weber's definition, according to which power is "the chance for one or several persons to assert their own will, without some social relation, against the resistance of other participants". It will be noted that this indicates a narrower interpretation of power as far as the concept of ownership-exercise is concerned; I exclude the power of objects or reified relations over man, or to use Marx's words, that "inhuman power which rules over the capitalist too".

The source of power is property; the source of property is power. The two viewpoints are sharply opposed to each other, and they are the expression of ideologies that have become political and material forces. Marx was faced with the problem that one of the most important outward forms of property relations as essential relations was the development of power relations. The answer which he gave to the question of the relationship between property and power, in his polemic with Heinzen, is still of importance for the sociological analysis of property relations. According to Marx, property relations have primacy over power:

"How the 'acquisition of money' changes into the 'acquisition of power' or 'property' into 'political domination', how between two kinds of power, instead of there being a firm difference (which Mr Heinzen sanctions as a *dogma*), there are on the contrary connections which go as far as being a union, of this Mr Heinzen may quickly convince himself if he takes a look at how the serfs *bought* their freedom, how the communes *bought* their municipal rights, how the bourgeois on the one hand wheedled the money out of the pockets of the feudal lords through trade and industry and changed their landed property into fleeting bills of exchange, and how on the other hand they helped the absolute monarchy to victory over the great feudal lords who had been thus undermined, and how they *bought* their titles from them."[33]

In Marx's analysis of *capitalist* society, the supreme problematic was indeed the process through which the "acquisition of money" turned into the acquisition of power, since the structure of capitalist society arose chiefly as a result of this process. But this in no way implies that the "acquisition of power" is then *free* from the "acquisition of money" (in this respect, it is relevant to recall the historical process through which the hierarchic order of the European feudal societies came into being). The mistake of the "official" marxism of the European social democratic parties consisted precisely in giving primacy to the property relations over the power relations in all circumstances, irrespective of the historical situation, on the assumption that the latter could always be "bought" by the proprietor. But this kind of mechanical view is far removed from Marx's attitude to history. Marx gave primacy to the property relations in the ontological sense, and above all in the historical emergence of capitalist property: "the political rule of the bourgeois class is a consequence of those modern production relations which are proclaimed as inevitable and eternal laws by the bourgeois economists".[34] It must not be forgotten, either, that in the polemic between Marx and Heinzen, power still appeared primarily as political or (in other words) administrative power, which in the form of the state was apparently entirely separate from the property relations. Marx obviously considered it his main task to demonstrate the dependence of the bourgeois "state", this apparently supreme power, on the property relations. He did not consider it worth debating whether property and power were identical or not: he called them a tautology, "which is already contained in the words themselves", but continually emphasised that even in its narrower sense, property was the direct or indirect source of power.

In the modern capitalist societies, the separation of property from power is not limited to politics but extends to almost every sphere of social and private life, and has become to a large extent a characteristic and economic administration too. In modern capitalism, the proprietor does not only acquire power through the state, which through various mechanisms is separate from him, but he also gives power to others in his own internal sphere, i.e. in the management of the enterprise. One of the phenomena which is most deserving of the attention of marxist analysis is this (partial) separation of property from power in the economic sphere; this is a conspicuous feature in the recent development of Western societies, and it marks them off not only from feudalism but also from classical capitalism. The intrusion of political power into the economic sphere (the state sector) means a certain separation between the essential owner, the capitalist state, and the institutions practising power (which belong to the category of ownership-exercise). And even if this does not change the dominant nature of bourgeois private property, it has brought about a very important modification in the property relations as essential relations, understood in Marx's terms, i.e. not divorced from the social relations but interpreted as an "organising principle".

Property and power over objects

Disposition over the objective relations of the production process forms an integral part of the exercise of property rights (or what I have termed "ownership-exercise"), and indicates first of all the determination of the structure of production (what shall be produced), the object of labour (what it shall be produced from), and the means of labour (how it shall be produced).

In pre-capitalist times the owner, or whoever personified him, was often faced with difficulties in his right of ownership-exercise, and was forced to transfer to others not only his power over people but also his power over objects. Typical cases of this were the "bureaucratic" empires of antiquity and China, where the ruler, personifying the ownership of the state, transferred these rights to a hierarchically ordered state administration. European feudalism provided a basically different solution to this problem: the *seigneur* and the landlord retained their power over their vassals and serfs, but transferred to them almost entirely the right of disposition over objects. It was precisely this kind of feudalism which made it possible for bourgeois private property to emerge, and thereby provided the opportunity for a dynamism of development that was unprecedented in history.

The principal moment in the development of bourgeois private property, besides this disposition over objects, was the achievement of power by the bourgeoisie over itself, which relatively quickly became power over others. It is no accident that the main protagonist in this process was precisely the serf who disposed of these objects. But with the development of bourgeois private property, the right to dispose of objects to others began to be transferred too; the first instance of this was the development of the joint stock company. Although every shareholder in the joint stock company actually disposes of his shares as his property, is entitled to appropriate the surplus value and may sell his shares at any time, the greater part of the ownership capacities nevertheless belong to enterprise management: the majority of shareholders are unable to participate in ownership-exercise, and often they do not even have real control over the enterprise management which acts in their name. However, the real managers of capitalist enterprises lead the masses of shareholders to believe that they are capable of exercising real control over the managers; this is a special domain in the management of capitalist enterprises, the domain of "expert manipulation". (American literature on management sociology provides innumerable examples of this: see, for example, Reinhard Bendix's *Work and Authority in Industry*.). The separation between the person of the proprietor and actual disposition over the relations of production also extends to the larger forms of private family property, and in this way the management apparatuses which have developed in the capitalist societies are able to exercise power (in the organisation of production) and possession (in the objective relations of production) at the same time. In modern capitalism, this has been added to by the increased importance of state property; this gives to certain state organs the kinds of jurisdiction which the administrations of capitalist enterprises have.

Property and disposition over the surplus product

There is a close historical link between property, on the one hand,

99

and disposition over the surplus product (the legal and practical capacity to appropriate it) on the other; this is one of the keys to the understanding of the property relations which exist in the current socialist societies. Ever since the possibility of producing a surplus product has existed, social struggles have in the last resort never been fought only for power or for disposition over the objective factors of production, but for the distribution of the surplus product; and the concrete property relations, power structures and various modes of ownership-exercise and possession have developed in this unceasing struggle.

In the course of history, disposition over the surplus product has not always belonged in the final analysis to the proprietor himself, because he has been forced to share this power of disposition either with authorities greater than himself (*seigneur*, monarch, etc.) or with those to whom he has transferred (in the sense mentioned above) his power of ownership over persons or over the objective factors of production. This means, of course, that not only is the actual right of disposition over the surplus product divided, but the surplus product itself is divided too. From this it also follows that the "division" is a permanent source of conflict between the groups taking part in ownership-exercise.

In classical capitalism, the capitalist himself by and large exercised the right to dispose of the surplus product, just as he held the power of disposition over persons and over the objective factors of production. But this independence was considerably clipped by developments in the last century. On the one hand the capitalist state has taken an increasingly active part in distributing the surplus value (either by siphoning it off or by direct intervention); and on the other hand, the managements of the capitalist enterprises have also been demanding to have a hand in it. (As many Western sociological studies can testify, managements are chiefly interested in the increase of reserve funds and investments, while the capitalists, especially the shareholders, are mainly interested in maximising dividends.)

The inheritance of property, its alienation, and control over possession

One of the most important elements in ownership-exercise is the inheritance and alienation of property, in which the property relations as essential social relations often attain their most pregnant form of expression. That is why I did not include this element in the notion of restricted possession which I applied to the other three capacities of ownership-exercise. The proprietor may transfer his personal power, the right of disposition over the objective conditions of production and the surplus product, or at least part of the latter; but if he renounces the right to alienate his property, he ceases to be a proprietor. On many occasions in history, however, these *sui generis* rights of the proprietor *as* proprietor have been restricted, in most cases in the name of some "collective" proprietor above him.

The proprietor's control over the possessor must be included among his *sui generis* rights. When we examine the exercise of any kind of power based on property relations and the various forms of ownership-exercise and possession, we must always ask whether there exists some kind of real control over those who dispose of power and exercise possession in the name of the proprietor. And if the answer is yes, we must examine how far this control extends, who or which groups exercise it, and what are the historical roots of their right and capacity to control.

The evolution of the forces of production and property relations

The multi-faceted theory of property relations which can be found in Marx's works has been deprived of its concrete nature by the schematism which has become dominant in marxist theory. It has been turned into the system of interconnections of some mystical power, which appears to rule over society as the laws of nature do over the material world. What has been obscured? The supreme importance of social struggle, in which the property relations assume their concrete form, and through which considerably differing types of ownership-exercise and possession develop, even at one and the same level of productive forces. Instead of supplying concrete historical analysis, the simplified conception of marxism has given rise to interpretations stating that the evolution of productive forces changes the property relations by the force of a law of nature, as it were. The necessary result of this view is overemphasis on the importance of the economic sphere, an overemphasis which a great number of marxists have long fought against, and notably Engels, Lukács and Gramsci. Berlinguer[35] draws attention to Togliatti's remarks about Gramsci, that "he never considered the economic structure to be a mysterious, hidden force from which the various situations developed automatically". Lenin himself was opposed to the "official" view on almost every

101

principal question of the strategy and structure of revolutionary social democracy. Although the October revolution was not only victorious over the bourgeoisie but also rendered palpably obsolete the ossification of marxism into a dogma, many of the tenets of this dogmatic marxism nevertheless lived on in the country where socialism had become victorious; it was now difficult not only to analyse the new phenomena in capitalism, but also to carry out any realistic self-analysis of the new socialist societies. We cannot yet give a satisfactory answer to the question of how and by what means, and under the influence of what social forces, schematism had become one of the main planks of official science in the USSR by the end of the twenties, reaching the text-books themselves during the thirties. It is impossible to ignore its influence on the stalinist theory of socialism, and especially on the tenets referring to property relations. The latter, especially where they touched on the new property relations, were considered irrevocable; their effect on ownership-exercise and possession made any realistic analysis extremely difficult, because the official viewpoint was protected by the severest clauses of the penal code against any attempt at confrontation, however justifiable this confrontation might be.

While this view of socialist property relations was ossified into a dogma for decades, the abolition of private property not only occurred in an increasing number of new countries but also took on increasingly varied forms. In such circumstances it has become a task of primary importance, not only for the social sciences but also for social practice, to examine the newly developed property relations without deliberately overlooking the power structures that have sprung up, the actual possibilities of possession, and the consequent power of disposition over the surplus product.

In this study, I am looking for an answer to these questions only in respect of the present conditions in the *European* socialist countries, and not of an analysis *in general* of every society that has abolished private property. I stress this because, in my view, all the historical conditions are now ripe for overcoming once and for all the idea that property relations, the forms of ownership-exercise and possession and of state organisations, must necessarily be *identical* in every respect in all societies which have abolished private ownership of the means of production, and that every deviation from this pattern is some sort of negative phenomenon. In our era we must also overcome the notion, which was dominant for a time and which in itself was already a way of correcting the "cult of personality" conception, that some variations which are a result of national characteristics can be recognised, but only within the scope of social laws that are considered to be generally and inevitably valid. In spite of the progressive role that this notion has played in the past, it allows no room for the possibility that different solutions may occur as the result of complex processes of social struggle, and thus that one alternative or another, all differing significantly from each other but all surpassing bourgeois private property to the same extent, may be equally victorious. At the moment, however, when this happens in practice, it is considered by the defenders of the first alternative to be a violation of socialist principles.

The new property relations as the negation of bourgeois private property

What we know of the property relations which have developed in the socialist societies of Europe consists first of all in a negation: there is no private property, or to put it more precisely, a new property relationship has been created by the abolition of bourgeois private ownership of the means of production, and by various methods such as nationalisation, mass collectivisation, etc. What this negation actually means can only be decided through a concrete analysis of reality; this is the only way we can find out how far and in what respects the new has in fact surpassed the old. History has seen many kinds of forces which are negative in their *effects*; however important the negation of the prevailing "establishment" may be at any given time, we certainly cannot identify it automatically with progress or with the quest for power. The question can only be answered if we first take account of the role which bourgeois private property has played in history.

The emergence of bourgeois private ownership of the means of production undoubtedly released powerful forces on to the historical scene, and it was mainly for this reason that mankind's progress began to accelerate at an unprecedented rate. Protestant "ethics" simply gave the ideological "green light" to the development of this form of ownership. I believe this needs stressing, because the dogmatic and simplified version of marxism often emphasises only the negative consequences of bourgeois private property: its anti-humanism, and its inability to function with optimum efficiency. This is dangerous not only because it gives a false view of the (past or present) world which maintains private property, but also because it impairs the realistic analysis of those property relations which prevail in socialism, and hampers any attempt to judge whether what has happened is more than a simple negation and whether it may be considered (and if so, in what sense) to actually surpass the previous conditions.

The importance of bourgeois private property in the development of the productive forces can best be measured by using the historical example which comes from comparing the Asiatic mode of production with post-Renaissance European development. In those countries where, as a result of various historical circumstances, the Asiatic mode of production became the prevailing form, the development of the more advanced forms of private property was blocked (the reasons for this have been analysed sufficiently in the existing literature); it was mainly for this reason that the development of the productive forces was interrupted for a period of centuries. The development of bourgeois private property in Europe, however, brought with it not only an economic dynamism which had been inconceivable in the preceding historical periods, but also social movements which expected the "common weal" to emerge from the abolition of private property and were ready to fight for this at whatever cost. From the eighteenth century onwards, Europe has been the scene of repeated social endeavours to replace private property with social forms of property, whether by means of specific social struggles or of utopian reforms. But however valuable these experiments have been for the history of mankind, in some way or other and after some period of time they have proved to be unviable. The same fate befell both Fourier's communistic communities and the noble ideas of the Paris Commune.

The overcoming of bourgeois private property has become a reality in our century, but it is far from being a historical necessity which occurs automatically. The progress of the productive forces and likewise of social relations has reached a level where it has become possible to dispense with and replace all the positive aspects which bourgeois property brought with it (and chiefly those to do with the dynamics of development), and to set in motion the kind of driving forces which were unable to evolve in the framework of private property. The relatively advanced level of the forces of production and of social relations in the twentieth century has enabled the previously anarchic and utopian socialist attempts at abolishing and surpassing bourgeois private property to develop into a force spanning the globe, which has now led to the development of new forms of government in many countries.

It follows from this that several kinds of state system may be built in accordance with the property relations which develop after the abolition of private property. Property relations never do determine the form of government unequivocally; this is valid not only for those societies built on private ownership of the means of production but also for the societies which surpass them. This is not because there are no extremely close links between the specific mode of ownership-exercise (the property relations as the outward form of the essential relations) and the state system. Rather, it is because after the abolition of private property, in systems of social economic management which differ according to the objective conditions of the society's existence and according to social struggles (i.e. the people who themselves make history), extremely varied forms have developed and will develop, both of ownership-exercise and of the state system.

This reveals itself in capitalism, too, although bourgeois private property is undoubtedly the dominant form which determines everything else. On the one hand there is a great variety of power structures and systems of siphoning off surplus value. On the other hand, it is also a fact that forms of ownership have developed or survived which differ essentially from each other in their mode of ownership-exercise (co-operative, institutional, state property, etc.); that is to say, here too we may distinguish to a considerable extent between different types of ownership-exercise and possession. When Marx, in his analysis of classical capitalism, foresaw the possibility of abolishing private property and emphasised the historical inevitability of this change, he also sensed that an evolution was taking place within capitalist property relations too; for example, he looked at the development of joint stock companies and at the emergence of various kinds of co-operative in this light. However, history has taken a course which differs considerably from Marx's prognosis. In the more advanced countries, capitalism has been able to adapt itself to the development of the productive forces better than Marx had assumed. Meanwhile the conditions for socialist revolution became ripe in the less advanced countries too, and because of the consistent struggle of the revolutionary forces and the historical circumstances, the overcoming of private property occurred here first.

The freeing of socialism from economic constraints

Many people, including friends of progress, have wondered whether the October revolution should not be considered a "momentary" success in marxist terms, one for which the economic preconditions were not entirely ripe, and where the material conditions for a new society really capable of surpassing capitalism had not yet come about. But we may also agree with Georg Lukács that the elimination of backwardness itself takes place in an essentially different way in socialist conditions from the way it occurs in capitalist conditions. In Lukács's view, socialism is capable of throwing off the fetters of narrow economic determination and of achieving something radically different, especially in the cultural sense: a more humane solution than that which is provided by the societies based on private property at a similar stage of economic development. But this capacity of socialism is the result of a historical process, and especially if the new order is victorious in a backward country, it can overcome economic constraint only at the expense of a long struggle. Marx often emphasised the role of historical constraint in this sense. He wrote that "people do not build themselves a new world out of 'earthly goods', as boorish superstition would have us believe, but out of the historical achievements of the vanishing worlds. In the course of their evolution they must first themselves *produce* the *material conditions* of a new society, and no effort of sentiment or will can free them from this fate."

Contrary to Marx's original concept, socialism triumphed in countries where not only was the level of production insufficient to serve as the material foundation for the "realm of freedom", but even the basic human necessities at subsistence level were not guaranteed. This fact had a great influence on the formation of property relations and the mode of ownership-exercise. Centralism, which penetrated right through the system of ownership-exercise in a relatively short time, was not brought about merely by some rationalising intention but was "enforced" by (a) the categorical need to conquer starvation, (b) the need to carry out rapid industrialisation and (c), last but not least, the equally pressing tasks of culture and education. But all these tasks, which were priorities for the Soviet Union in the twenties and are now priorities for present-day China, are passing phenomena, and in the European socialist countries they have already become more or less a thing of the past.

The level which these countries have reached in terms of the per capita income means that the conquest of starvation and poverty in the traditional sense is no longer society's main task in the sphere of consumption. In its place, the task arises of developing a pattern of culture which opens up greater possibilities for the realisation of socialist values than have been achieved in the advanced capitalist societies at the same level*. And in the sphere of production, now that backwardness has been eliminated and the task of extensive industrialisation solved, the main issue has become the effective utilisation of the available labour and, through this, the development of a greater dynamism than is generally characteristic of those capitalist countries which have reached a similar level. The cultural task too, which in Marx's opinion had been one of the main historical functions of centralism in the absolute monarchies, has been essentially solved, since illiteracy has in general been overcome, a basic seven or eight years' education made universal, the mass communications media extended, a certain minimum level of health ensured, etc. Therefore the task for today and for the immediate future is to raise the cultural level further, so that it affords greater opportunities on the one hand for the development of the individual, and on the other for the increased democratisation of society.

All this means that today in the final analysis, the European socialist societies are already in a position to free themselves from the oppressive economic constraints on their social relations, and to develop them more freely. But these societies can avail themselves of this freedom only if they are capable of critically analysing their actual conditions, in particular the existing property relations, and of surpassing the dominant ideological and legal abstractions in this latter case. Not even in class societies did Marx consider the existing state and political machinery to be incapable of changing itself. He wrote that "when the essential material conditions of society have developed to the extent where the transformation of its official political constitution has become a vital necessity, the entire face of the old political power changes. Thus for instance, at this stage the absolute monarchy tries to *decentralise* instead of *centralising*, which is its proper civilising activity."

What, then, is to stop us from believing that the political power in socialist societies is much more profoundly capable of renewing itself?

The standard "histmat" view of socialist property relations

The standard "histmat" view presents a very simplified picture

---

* See Andras Hegedus and Maria Markus: "The Choice of Alternatives and Values in the Long-Range Planning of Distribution and Consumption" in *The Humanisation of Socialism* (London, Allison & Busby, 1976).

of socialist property relations, a picture that is purged of any actual ownership-exercise or possession. It is mainly this that separates this simplifying trend from the traditionally creative methods of historical materialism*. The "histmat" view recognises the socialist character of two forms of property: co-operative and state property. "Socialist state property and co-operative property are of the same type," writes a Hungarian textbook, "they are the direct unions of the producers and of the means of production on the basis of collective ownership of the means of production." The same idea has been formulated even more explicitly by Karoly Foldes: "The members of society are direct producers individually, and in their entirety are the proprietors of the means of production". This is, as we shall see, the usual abstract formulation. Let us see what the author means by this, when he speaks of socialist property not in general but in terms of its two basic forms: "Between the two forms of property there are *also* differences. While the product of the state enterprises is *the property of the whole people*, the co-operative enterprise and its products belong in essence to its members." [My emphasis—*A.H.*]

We can see in this formulation a distinction is made between the two types of collective ownership (public/national and co-operative/group property) without, however, the author asking in either case what relations of ownership-exercise or possession have developed, and who or which group *actually* dispose of the different forms of ownership-exercise. In order to demonstrate that this "histmat" view is still far from having been overcome, I have consciously chosen a recently published textbook and another recently published monograph. In this conception, the problem of property is summed up as a single task: to raise co-operative (group) property to a higher level, i.e. to the state (public) level. At one time the "histmat" view considered this to be a social condition for a higher order, an important precondition for the achievement of communism.

In Yugoslavia at the end of the 1940s a forceful critique, stimulated by the well-known political conflict, was developed to counter this ideological abstraction of socialist property relations. To solve the problem of ownership which was raised in this critique, the Yugoslav marxists worked out the "self-management" theory; and in putting this into practice, they carried out an essential

---

* See Andras Hegedus and Maria Markus: "Tendencies in Marxist Sociology in the Socialist Countries", in *The Humanisation of Socialism* (London, 1976).

change in the mode of ownership-exercise, and thus in the property relations as essential social relations. The means of production have legally become the property of the collective of workers and employees in the enterprise, and the apparatus which fulfils the function of technical and economic management is appointed and controlled by the workers or by organs elected by them at all levels of what one might call the hierarchy. For the adherents of the self-management theory, the problem of property means the consistent realisation of the self-management principle and the overcoming of the strong "bureaucratic tendencies". They believe that this problem can be solved "completely" after many decades have passed, mainly through a considerable increase in economic development and in the standard of living and culture.

Those who support the first alternative believe that the property relations which have arisen in Yugoslavia have replaced public or "real socialist" property with a retrograde form, with group property. We can even find people who believe that the changes which have occurred there are equivalent to a restoration of capitalism. The defenders of Yugoslav practice, however, consider this form of property to be the only possible form of socialist property in present-day conditions, and reject the notion that there is any other possibility that might correspond to the requirements of socialism. Although we have to accept both *basic* types of socialist property as realities, this in no way means that we must also accept the either/or alternative. In my opinion, the apologists for both solutions make their judgements in an arbitrary way, mainly because they fail to analyse the actual consequences of the property relations in the form of property which they defend. They only attempt to do so through the form of property which they criticise; thus, in general, there is more truth in their critique than in their views on what they consider to be the positive solution.

A dilemma: possession by the state administration and ownership-exercise by society as a whole

Taking all this as our point of departure, we can make a distinction among the following main forms of ownership-exercise or possession (i.e. restricted ownership): (a) possession by the state administration; (b) ownership-exercise by society as a whole; (c) possession by the managerial administration of the enterprise or institution; (d) ownership-exercise by the enterprise or institution collective; (e) associated ownership-exercise; and (f) private

109

or family ownership-exercise and possession. In my opinion, what the type of ownership-exercise and possession signifies is an analytical category, serving primarily to describe the realm of phenomena. In this sense, I do not think it possible, simply without any further explanation, to identify these types with the property relations themselves, as essential social relations, or with the co-operative and state (etc.) forms of ownership in which *various* types of ownership-exercise or possession may be discerned. In introducing the categories of ownership-exercise and possession (the latter indicating the disposition over power and the surplus product), I am attempting to cast doubt on the abstract legal and ideological treatment of property relations, and to replace them with a concrete sociological analysis.

When I speak about possession by the state administration, I mean the situation in which the organs of state administration have the legal and practical capacity for power over people and objects and have disposition over the surplus product. In the direct central planning system this type was characteristic not only of state property in the narrower sense but also of the sphere of industrial and agricultural co-operatives. In the new system of economic management, on the other hand (contrary to the generally held view), it is not usually asserted even with regard to state enterprises.

Possession by the state administration is an increasingly widespread form in capitalist societies too, where it is a characteristic practice of some state enterprises. As Istvan Gergely wrote in a recent book: "Some of the state enterprises, although they function in the form of an enterprise, are essentially state institutions, closely linked to the state and the state budget, with only very limited financial, economic and political independence: for example, French Radio and Television or the Post Office. The majority of these do not pay any taxes, their expenses are covered from the state budget, and their income is paid into the Exchequer."[36] The increase of state enterprises in capitalist societies (which takes place especially in capital-intensive branches of industry) strengthens not only possession by the state administration but also, as we shall see later, possession by the managerial administration of enterprises or institutions. Both forms, however, are integral parts of a state which has the maintenance of private property as one of its main functions.

For those societies which have overcome private property, the state administration type of possession undoubtedly has great and as yet not fully exploited advantages in a certain historically determined period (as long as it does not exceed the desirable level),

110

not only for the dynamic development of economic life but also for the realisation of socialist goals. But in spite of all its practical advantages, if we set out from the real conditions, it cannot by itself be considered to constitute ownership-exercise by the whole of the people or by society as a whole. Its total societal character can only be realised to the extent that the state administration, which exercises rights of property, is under actual and effective social control. In this sense, possession by the state can increasingly become ownership-exercise by the people as a whole, i.e. it can become societal ownership-exercise, but only through the strengthening of democratic forms of administration. It can scarcely be denied that this process cannot yet be considered finished and closed in any socialist country, nor that the possibility of continuing this process by force (as one of the realistic alternatives of progress) is excluded in any socialist country.

It follows from this that state ownership in the socialist countries in its present form cannot be considered as bureaucratic state ownership without any further analysis, because the possibility exists for society, through various mechanisms, to exercise a certain control over the administrative institutions of possession, even under the present circumstances. That is why I do not speak about ownership-exercise by the state administration but about possession by it. The realisation of this possibility takes place by means of social struggles. There are forces which seek to stiffen the bureaucratic forms of administration, which seek to make the social character of ownership-exercise a purely formal one, and which thus try to transform possession into ownership-exercise. At the same time, the nature of the system and the negation of private ownership of the means of production create an increasingly strong movement to make ownership-exercise genuinely social. The existence of these opposing forces or tendencies, and the struggle between them, can clearly be observed in the majority of the European socialist countries. The common focal point of this struggle, the core of the problem of property in the European socialist countries is, with the exception of Yugoslavia, the replacement of possession by the state administration with ownership-exercise by society as a whole.

Possession by the state administration can be clearly recognised in its exercise of power over people and objective relations and in its disposition over the surplus product. It reveals characteristics which are different from other types of ownership-exercise and possession. *Power* is hierarchically arranged, with the relations of sub- and super-ordination forming an unbroken chain from the

111

highest organ of state administration to the point of execution. The extent of the dependence among the various levels of sub- and super-ordination moves along an extraordinarily broad scale: from technical dependence, which is a relatively balanced, mutual dependence between subordinates and superiors, to personal dependence, in which mutuality ceases and the subordination of the lower ranks to their superiors becomes almost unlimited. To those who are on the higher level this relationship often appears to be extremely efficient, because there is less uncertainty, less arbitrary changing of the place of employment, etc. The objective conditions of personal dependence develop where individuals have no possibility of changing their place of employment for another one affording identical prestige and income, and when one or another of these criteria (or both) are of vital existential importance to the individual. (During the period of the personality cult, a much harsher form of personal dependence existed: in addition to the existential and financial forms of compulsion, fear and terror became one of the main instruments of the exercise of power.)

Disposition over "objects", like the exercise of power, takes place within a hierarchically arranged decision-making system. The main framework for the exercise of this right is the direct stipulations of the plan, by which the highest organs of state administration determine all the changes that are to be made in the structure of production down to the finest details; it also decides about the distribution of investment among the various sectors of society and branches of the economy, even among enterprises, and thus about all the important questions of economic development. Directing the economy and to some extent the whole of social life by means of the decisions of the state administration undoubtedly has, as I have already said, many advantages, but at the same time it creates great difficulties. Economic analyses have criticised these negative economic consequences satisfactorily from the standpoint of efficiency, and it would therefore be superfluous for me to deal with this here. I should simply like to emphasise that in my opinion, if we compare this form to that of possession by the managerial administration of the enterprises (or institutions), then from the standpoint of optimisation it undoubtedly proves the more advantageous choice in many branches (for example, railways, the post office, electricity generation, etc.), while in many others it is the less advantageous one.

The connection between possession by the state administration and disposition over the surplus product is much less disputed. With possession by the state administration, the siphoning off and distribution of a certain part of the surplus product, like all the other forms of decision-making which have been discussed, takes place within the hierarchy of the state administration, and in an even more centralised form than in the previous cases. But we must make one reservation. The almost unlimited right of disposition over the surplus product, which is controlled almost solely within the administrative organisation, does not mean the right to unrestricted individual appropriation. The hierarchic differentials in income that occur in the state administration in the socialist countries are incomparably smaller (even in those places where the differentials are the biggest) than those which exist in the state administrative apparatus of the societies built on private property.

Possession by the state administration becomes ownership-exercise by society as a whole (where this notion is limited to organisations forming a state) at the point where actual social control is achieved over those organs of state administration which exercise possession in regard to state property, and to the extent that these administrative organs depend for their existence on those organisations and movements which carry out the rule of society as a whole. Consequently, the reinforcement of the public nature of ownership-exercise, where possession itself is exercised by the state administration, essentially depends on solving the highly complex problem of social control over the various institutions of state administration, a problem which today is expressed in practice mainly through attempts at democratising the socio-political system.

It does not lie within the scope of this study to describe this highly complex social movement and its struggle. I simply wish to *illustrate* the problem by raising one question (and only in part), that of Parliament. A very important aspect of this movement is the struggle to transfer some of the decisions concerning the right to ownership-exercise to the representative organs of society such as Parliament. But this is an effective solution only if the following conditions are fulfilled: (a) if the representative organ's decisions will mean that choices are made between real alternatives, and not simply that the proposals of the administration will be adopted with a few insignificant amendments; (b) if it becomes possible for social public opinion to acquaint itself with all the important questions of economic development, so that it can have a direct effect on decisions taken in Parliament or in the municipal councils; (c) if the principle of incompatibility is asserted in the composition of Parliament and the municipal councils (i.e. people with positions of responsibility in the administration cannot also be members of parliament or of the councils); (d) if the members of parliament

113

and of the councils can rely not only on public opinion but also on the views of those experts whose livelihood is not dependent on the administration. These are only a few of the preconditions, which we can already sense today, for the achievement of social control over the administration. Similar problems occur in the councils, at all levels. Real social control over the administration can, however, become effective if there is a real and widespread social movement which struggles in practice for these aims and in which, however, new problems will certainly arise.

All this indicates that we must not simply *reject* the state administration's justification for exercising possession. We must attempt to *surpass* it, to enhance its social character in those decisions which are connected with ownership, so that public ownership-exercise becomes a reality. (I use the expression "ownership-exercise" here because it is not like the case of state administration, which involves possession, i.e. a restricted exercise of ownership: the owner or proprietor here is, in the last analysis, society as a whole, the public.) In my opinion, this is a realistic alternative for progress, which can keep the advantages of possession by the state without rigidly bureaucratic power relations congealing. In the socialist societies, possession by the state administration historically precedes ownership-exercise by society as a whole, and the progressive character of the former consists chiefly in its preparation for the latter.

But the path outlined above (the replacement of possession by the state administration with ownership-exercise by society as a whole) is only one of the possible alternatives. It is by no means certain that this solution will be victorious in the struggle of social forces everywhere. The possibility cannot be excluded that, at least in some countries, possession by the state administration will be frozen for decades, and will remain the principal and all-determining form of ownership-exercise. Each type of ownership-exercise and possession that we have discussed so far (both the state administrative type and the putative public type) is enclosed within a *national* framework. The experience of recent decades has proved that private property moves across national boundaries more easily than possession by the state administration. This causes conflicts, especially in those socialist countries where this form of ownership-exercise plays an extremely important role and also to a large extent determines political decisions. For this reason, politics may easily become subordinate to the interests involved in national property; this form of possession can thus become an almost insurmountable obstacle to the movement of concentrated capital across national boundaries, even though this kind of internationalisation is in some dynamic sectors of industry an indispensable precondition for a more rapid development towards international standards.

A further dilemma: possession by the enterprise administration and ownership-exercise by the enterprise collective

Possession by the managerial administration of the enterprise or institution is a rapidly advancing form in socialist reality, but conscious acceptance of it is a highly problematical question. (I revert here to the term "possession" because in this case ownership-exercise is necessarily restricted from several angles: from possession by the state administration, from ownership-exercise by society as a whole or by the enterprise collective.)

"Possession by the managerial administration of the enterprise" may seem the most scandalous of all the expressions used in this study. This may well be where the various predominating views will clash most sharply, because neither the defenders of the stalinist theory of the state nor those of the Yugoslav self-management system will accept its validity. But whatever opinions are voiced from either side, this type of possession nonetheless exists. The hierarchically ordered managerial apparatus in economic enterprises or institutions exercises its possession in the field of property with a relatively high degree of independence. Institutional possession occurs partly as a *negation* of the state administration, either on the basis of a practical critique in ideological or political terms (as in Yugoslavia), or of an approach which stresses efficiency (as in the case of the economic reforms in the European socialist countries in recent years); it can partly be found in the co-operative where it indicates that ownership-exercise by the state administration is still incomplete.

The Yugoslav self-management theory was formulated in 1950. It condemned possession by state management as a bureaucratic distortion of socialism, and wanted to replace it with the "ownership of associated producers". However, the form of property which the Yugoslav self-management system has developed cannot unconditionally be considered social property, as the defenders of self-management assert. In Yugoslav enterprises management and therefore possession inevitably get into the hands of a separate apparatus; the control of this apparatus by the collective often becomes purely formal, not only because *management* does not

115

wish to share power but also because a considerable number of the collective *do not themselves feel interested* in the enterprise's activity as a whole, and continue to think and feel not as associated proprietors but as wage workers, in spite of workers' self-management. The institutional character of ownership-exercise may have been strengthened by the fact that, for various reasons, the movement for the achievement of societal rule has in fact slackened and become purely formal. And in contemporary societies, the achievement of societal rule is not a state of affairs but a permanent struggle.

There is a similar situation in the co-operatives in the European socialist countries outside Yugoslavia. Self-management exists here too in theory, and is declared to exist in law. The co-operatives dispose not only of means provided by the state but also of considerable co-operative funds. However, this latter is the property of the institution; when they increase, the individual member only gets an individual benefit at the end of a particular year when this has been reflected in the net income of the co-operative, i.e. in the value of the work unit. It therefore follows that the main interest of the members of the co-operative is to maximise their individual income (which in fact has the character of wages), and it is no accident that at least in a considerable number of co-operatives there is pressure to introduce the form of wages which is applied in the state enterprises, and to make incomes as stable and predictable as possible. In this situation, the general trend in most co-operatives is to reduce investments to the lowest possible level and to distribute as great a part of the collective income as possible in dividends per work unit. In every socialist country that has carried out a mass collectivisation of agriculture (and not only in Hungary), a law has had to be passed to counter this trend, so that there is a fixed minimum investment ratio. It should be noted that the Yugoslav economy has been struggling against similar difficulties for almost two decades; there too, the worker in an enterprise is primarily interested in maximising his wages and not in making the sacrifices that will turn the enterprise into a prosperous one.

The main obstacle to possession by the collective of the enterprise or institution is that the majority of workers and employees in socialist enterprises, and even the members of the co-operatives, continue to consider themselves as wage workers. This is because the rights of ownership, which they have at their disposal as citizens of the state and as members of the collective of the given enterprise, are abstract; the results of rational management of the property are expressed only in wages (or in the share of profit linked

116

with wages), and even this often involves a series of transmissions so complex that they are difficult to see through. In this situation it would seem to be natural for a large number of workers and employees to retain the typical wage worker's mentality; they endeavour to maximise their wages and to minimise their work performance. It is because of this situation that we see well-known practices such as the withholding of performance when norms are readjusted—entire collectives often not only tolerate this but expressly demand it from their members.

Where an economic (market) price can be introduced in place of the previous bureaucratic price (which was fixed by the decision-making system of state management), the new system of economic management again strengthens possession by the enterprise or institution. In these enterprises it becomes possible for expert management to make the decisions concerning all the important questions of enterprise development (changes in the product structure, technical development, investment, etc.). The replacement of possession by state management with possession by enterprise management is, of course, a process that is accompanied by sharp conflicts. Those organs of state administration which have exercised possession up to that point do everything in their power to maintain their old policies, even if perhaps in a changed form and at the expense of a considerable amount of decentralisation; this means that we are far from being able to observe the replacement of one form of possession with another in every case.

The determination of the proper ratio between possession by state management and by enterprise management is actually a problem of optimisation, if we disregard those particular interests which seek to make one or the other form absolute. The question, properly formulated, is as follows: what type, or what ratio of the two types, is the most favourable in various branches of industry? If a one-sided priority is given to either of the solutions and the concrete conditions are overlooked, this may lead to a considerable reduction in efficiency. This also means, in my opinion, that neither type of possession is "more socialist" than the other: it is simply that in certain branches and developmental situations, one is more efficient and yields better results than the other.

The situation is entirely different if we contrast possession by state management with possession by the enterprise collective. The question of efficiency may be specifically raised here too (and the answer may vary a great deal, depending on the historical situation). But it is not so decisive as the objective of humanisation, which unequivocally puts ownership-exercise by the whole of

117

society above possession by the state administration, and that of the collective above the enterprise management. With possession by state management, the problem is to strengthen society's control and thereby to give ownership a public character, so that society as a whole, and especially those people who directly carry out the production or the services, are interested in it. And with possession by enterprise management, the perspective of socialist development demands first of all that the collective of workers and employees should control management more effectively, and that through this, institutional managerial possession should be replaced by collective group ownership. In our present conditions a greater legal opportunity for this exists in the co-operatives, but in practice it may be easier to achieve in state enterprises, where the workers' collective is culturally more advanced and more experienced in political activity, and where it is therefore in a better position to exercise actual social control over the institution's hierarchically ordered management. The construction of a system of supervisory boards for the enterprises may become a very effective instrument for achieving this purpose.

A contribution to overcoming possession by enterprise management would also be made by increasing the element of individual interest in the production and service collectives in a new and more practical way. In my opinion it would be possible, without violating the principles of either socialism or optimisation, to create a new form of social property which so far has not been accepted in socialism: group property, as partial property. This form of property would be created by the investments which enterprises and co-operatives supply out of their own assets; the *size* of these enterprise investments could be regulated by various economic measures (rates of taxation and interest, rules governing the repayment of credits etc.). The enterprise's investments would become the possession (in the form of shares) of those who during the given period have contributed their labour to the creation of the financial preconditions for the investment. In accordance with prescribed rules, the workers and employees would be entitled to choose whether they wanted to receive their portion of the profits in money or in shares. The enterprises would of course have to pay dividends on these shares, and care would have to be taken that the workers could redeem the shares at the enterprise where they receive them (with certain restrictions). Thus the workers and employees of the enterprise would be individually interested in the investments, inasmuch as the enterprise should be able not only to maintain but to increase its assets through good management, which would be the only way of maintaining and regularly increasing the value of the shares. If the enterprise is managed badly, the first assets to be put at risk are its own, i.e. the money of those who created the new value in the preceding period through their labour in the enterprise.

This new and practical alternative form of property would make the workers and employees interested in the activity of the enterprise and in the practical realisation of ownership-exercise by the collective, not simply as wage earners but as part owners too (this goes beyond the current profit-sharing system). This would have a particularly compelling influence on those who have worked in the enterprise for a longer period and have thus accumulated a larger number of shares. This solution would to some extent alleviate the current problem with pensioners (although this is only a secondary result); first of all, those who have worked for a longer time and possess more shares would obtain a certain quantity of dividends, and secondly they would thus continue to be interested in the activity of the enterprise and retain their links with social production.

This form of property would change the position of enterprise management in many respects. For one thing, it would make management easier. Although the difference would not be noticeable from year to year, the strengthening consciousness of "it's our property" would make discipline and organisation easier; the role of administrative disciplinary measures would be reduced, and the collective itself would take a more forceful stand against those who disrupt the organisation of the work process. But an even bigger influence on management would be the fact that the latter would be responsible not only to the higher organs but also to its own workers and employees, since it would be managing considerable sums of theirs. Bad management, therefore, would no longer simply entail disciplinary measures from above (which in any case can often be evaded or rendered purely formal, by having "connections in the right places") but would also rouse the anger of workers whose individual material interests had been damaged. The new system of economic management has already brought about this kind of responsibility in part; but in this case it is workers' wage increases that are put at risk (though this risk is considerably reduced by having wide opportunities for changing one's place of work). But if the risk is extended beyond the workers' wages to their "shares", the enterprise management would be forced to inform the workers in as much detail as possible and to ask their opinion before taking any important step, since other-

119

wise they would have to accept an intolerably heavy responsibility.

This solution can be used in the co-operatives too, of course, since at the moment there is no genuine part ownership in the co-operatives either; for the reasons outlined above, members of the co-operatives consider themselves wage workers rather than part owners. State property, state credit, investments out of state assets, etc., naturally play a role in the co-operatives too. But the new form of social property could be strengthened by investments from the co-operative's own assets, so that there are increased opportunities for developing collective ownership-exercise. This kind of solution naturally has many other consequences, not only in economic but in political life. But I believe it would have more positive than negative effects.

Furthermore, we cannot underestimate the influence which this new form of property, with its strengthening of ownership-exercise by the enterprise collective, would have on the workers of the advanced capitalist countries. The apologists for capitalism have long been proclaiming the idea of a people's capitalism, but it is a well-known fact that only a fragment of the working class have become possessors of shares in the capitalist countries, and even this has only been in insignificant quantities. With the solution which I put forward, workers and employees in the socialist enterprise would gradually become the actual owners of a certain part of the assets which they have accumulated.

It will be asked, of course, whether this is not a return to some kind of capitalist solution. The opponents of this new form of property can obviously make use of this argument, since the shares do in fact resemble shares as they exist in the capitalist countries. But in spite of the formal resemblance, it is a different solution, for two main reasons. First of all, the shares could only be obtained through work, whereas the wealth of the capitalists has not been accumulated through their work but through their exploitation of workers. Those who attack this new form of property by alleging that it is capitalism would have to go all the way with their argument and state that capital is created by capitalists' work. In the second place, partial property would be an organic part of the socialist system, a form *complementary* to existing socialist public and state property. Ownership-exercise by the enterprise collective would only be possible in that part of the economy where ownership-exercise by state management or by the people as a whole does not offer an effective solution even at today's level of the productive forces.

Associated ownership-exercise and associated possession

So far, I have emphasised the fact that a special management apparatus must necessarily have some part in exercising the power that is linked with property, in exercising *possession*, and in disposing of the surplus product, even where *ownership-exercise* is by society or the collective. But we need not exclude the possibility that in certain spheres self-management may be carried out in the full, strict sense of the term, with the collective exercising all the decision-making rights that are associated with the exercise of ownership. I term this "associated ownership-exercise" or, where it is severely curtailed by outside institutions, associated possession. At the moment this solution occurs relatively rarely in practice; it exists mainly in lower-ranking co-operatives, in which the act of association does not cover the entire productive activity of its members but is usually directed at the solution of some special task. But we cannot exclude the possibility that in the future, the scope for associated possession in this sense will be extended*. Associated possession may develop in various small-scale work organisations (e.g. squads of tractor drivers), but here too this has to be largely subordinate to other forms of exercise of ownership. I therefore consider "possession" to be the more apt expression in this case.

The various types of private ownership-exercise and private possession, and their role in socialist societies

Small-scale private property, affording only very limited opportunities for exploitation, play an important part in socialist societies almost everywhere. This is especially so in agriculture, not only for the optimisation of this sphere but also for human reasons. There are many indications that membership of an agricultural co-operative does not exclude the ambition to own land. In recent years there has been an increase in the buying and selling of land in several countries. Outside the agricultural sphere, private property has been spreading especially in the form of owning homes and plots of land, and in this respect too its role seems to be increasing rather than decreasing. Private property must not, however, be identified with ownership-exercise and possession by

---

* See Andras Hegedus and Maria Markus: "Collectivity and Individuality" in *The Humanisation of Socialism* (London, 1976).

private persons or families, because state property (e.g. in some forms of retail trade and service) and co-operative property (some household plots) can both serve as a basis for private possession.

For the purposes of this essay we are not interested so much in the fact itself that private property exists, but rather in the extent and actual function of private ownership-exercise, and especially of private possession. We may distinguish the following three main types of private possession, on the basis of the function of private production or servicing units: (a) an independent production or servicing unit whose products are commodities, and which is in some kind of direct contact with the consumer; (b) a production or servicing unit which is vertically integrated into a larger economic unit (the link with the larger unit may lie either in the production or servicing process, or in commodity exchange, or in both); (c) a private or family production or servicing activity which satisfies the person's or family's own consumption.

The household plot may also fulfil differing functions, which in turn have an influence on the nature of ownership-exercise or possession. In a previous book I distinguished between three historical and still extant types of household plots: (a) those producing for the free market (the object is commodity production, but the producer is in direct contact with the consumer); (b) those connected with a larger commercial or productive concern; (c) those practising subsistence economy (the family producing for its own needs). As we can see, this is essentially the same typology as that which applies to private property in general. The types which are constructed in this way, and which may now be considered historically developed, differ considerably as regards the mode of ownership-exercise or possession.

The extent of private (family) ownership-exercise and possession is severely limited in almost every socialist country. The power derived from this type of property may only spread to a relatively small number of people, and even this power is effectively limited by various measures. But at the same time, monopoly situations often provide wide-scale opportunities for appropriating the surplus product (and even surplus profit), because of very limited supply in relation to demand. This, and not the weakness of administrative measures, is the main reason why some of those with private ownership-exercise or possession—especially craftsmen and retailers—appear to public opinion to be an enviable stratum, enjoying outstanding financial success. And in agriculture, one also has to note the existence of a stable stratum which has private ownership-exercise or possession of production for the market, especially on the peripheries (e.g. wine-growing, early-crop fruits and vegetables, etc.). But the production and services involved here are based to a much greater extent on the proprietor's (or his family's) own labour than they are in industry and commerce: that is to say, the opportunities for appropriating the surplus product produced by others is much more limited.

Some extraordinarily interesting problems are raised by the second type of private production or servicing, and their importance is far from being fully recognised. The second type is the private or family economic unit which is vertically integrated into state or co-operative enterprises. This will perhaps play an outstanding part in the future, especially in agriculture and in certain parts of the service sector. It has many disadvantages, but there are also advantages; it can hardly be denied that in certain spheres it offers the most favourable solution not only from the viewpoint of optimisation but also from that of humanisation. Its advantage over the first type of private production or servicing is that it fits organically into the production of society as a whole, and those who exercise the rights of ownership or possession have no opportunity to appropriate the surplus product produced by others; it is usually, of course, the organs of state or enterprise management which decide about the surplus product in this case.

In evaluating this type, however, the important fact should be noted that disposition over the surplus product takes place in this case according to general criteria, and not according to an evaluation of the labour of the individual, which is inseparable from his personality. The result is that whatever the wider interconnections of this kind of private economic unit may be, it is not subordinated to the hierarchy of the management apparatus in the way that workers and employees of enterprises and institutions are when state or enterprise management exercises possession. In cases where there are no great advantages in efficiency to be gained from having a big concentration of production or services, this solution —the vertical integration of private production or servicing—provides at least as great a contribution to humanisation as *simple* co-operation does. However, one must not idealise this type and present it as an approximation to socialist ideals—for the simple reason, even if there is no other, that it encloses the working activity of the individual within the framework of a private economic unit, the family, and thereby hinders the development of his personality. But neither is simple co-operation, at the expense of efficiency, the only path open for a socialist development of the vertically integrated exercise of private ownership or possession, for it is also possible that the individual units within the vertical integration can become closely linked and make use of the various forms of co-operation and social control too.

The subsistence economy, production for the family's own needs, creates far fewer social problems, and the extent of it is constantly being reduced by the progress of commodity relations. It makes Stalin's ideas about the household plot (the sole justification was its satisfaction of the agricultural family's own needs) completely obsolete.

Perspectives for solving the problem of property

Two tendencies may be observed in the development of socialism, contradicting each other and also contradicting, in an especially acute manner, the "political economy" of socialism: (a) the character of labour as *individual* property is strengthening, and all the bureaucratic barriers which have systematically restricted the *individual* ownership of labour are slowly being removed; and (b) the opportunities are steadily increasing for the individual person, who under socialism is ultimately the free owner of his own labour, not only to sell it as a commodity but also to assert his potential rights as its owner. It seems that the overcoming of capitalism by socialism does not occur through the abolition of the commodity nature of labour. Rather, on the one hand labour as a commodity achieves free development in relation to possession by state management and enterprise or institutional management; while on the other hand, the owners of labour (as potential owners of the means of production) are also increasingly able to achieve effective social rule over the special management apparatuses which dispose of the capacity to exercise possession—and, as a result of this, various types of social ownership-exercise develop and may become dominant.

If we reject the interpretation of socialism as a constant state of affairs and consider it as a process, the forward goal of social progress cannot just be the improvement of material well-being; it must be, through the increase in the productivity of labour, the liberation of man from all personal and alienated power. The transition to this, which will probably encompass many generations, appears to demand some kind of social control (and this, too, is not conceived as a permanent state of affairs) in which individuals, as members of various social collectives and movements, can exercise social rule over those who dispose of power over them in any sense.

In my opinion, it is beyond all doubt that there exists no single monolithic solution to the contemporary property problems of the European socialist societies, i.e. that it is impossible to make any one form of property (or ownership-exercise, or possession) general and exclusive. Even if it were possible, it would not be desirable from the standpoint either of optimisation or of humanist values. Even after the property problems of today have been solved, types of ownership-exercise which differ essentially from each other will continue to exist: (a) ownership-exercise by society as a whole, by means of actual control over state management; (b) ownership-exercise by the enterprise collective, by means of control by the workers' and employees' collective over the special management apparatus of the enterprise; (c) smaller associations of producers developing within the above framework; (d) simple (family) commodity production or servicing units, integrated into larger economic units, in which the integration is assisted by forms of co-operative and social control.

This is, of course, a long way from what might be considered the complete liberation of man, the arrival of the realm of freedom. But Marx did not consider this to be something that was realisable in the near future. As he wrote in *The Civil War in France:*

> "The working class does not expect wonders from the Commune. It has no ready-made utopias which can be introduced *par décret du peuple*. It knows that until it can achieve its own liberation and, together with this, the higher form towards which present society is irresistibly advancing by means of its active economic forces, it has to pass through a whole series of long struggles and historic processes which will change both the circumstances and the people."

In the light of the long and uninterrupted struggles which humanity faces (even if this process does not occur without suffering relapses), it is becoming increasingly justifiable to give an affirmative answer to Gramsci's question about whether "man can be the master of his own fate, and form and create his own life". And this question will be decided chiefly by which of the currently possible alternatives in the development of property relations is realised.

VIII: Lenin and the Alternative Types of Socialist Economy

I do not consider the writing of essays for anniversaries to be the most enviable of tasks, especially when it is in memory of a man such as Lenin. The various forms of his deification, the assertions of his infallibility and his capacity to foresee everything, can only belittle his greatness, his truly human nature. He was the most influential moulder of a period that was of great importance for mankind, and if we want to follow in his steps, we must above all understand the period on which his work—his activity in the fields of practice and theory—left their indelible traces.

The most significant period of his life was the five years following the October revolution in which, as leader of the victorious revolution and in perpetual confrontation with a reality that posed thousands of problems, he laid the initial foundations of the theory of a new social order. One of the most important parts of this theoretical basis was the views he developed about the socialist economy. In the following pages my main aim will be to sketch out briefly the ideas he developed in connection with the theme of administration. My intention is not, however, to provide a collection of quotations which could be considered valid from Lenin's day until the present. Such an exercise, as experience shows, can serve to justify any number of different views from all sorts of positions. Rather, I attempt to understand Lenin's way of thinking as a true revolutionary in this important complex of themes.

A survey of the historical circumstances under which the Soviet state formed its economic administration can serve as a contribution to the debate that has developed on the issue of the administration in the socialist countries; a debate which has been going on for decades at both the ideological and the practical level with unrelenting vehemence. In order to understand any given phenomenon, one must study its process of origin and return to it *in statu nascendi*. Precisely because of this, in this question as with many others in the theory of socialism, we can learn a lot from those years in which a choice was made between historically real alternatives; or to put it another way, when different paths of development were still open.

In the Soviet Union the construction of the administration came to manifest itself most significantly in economic life, and precisely in this respect a historically new phenomenon came on to the scene which had never been experienced before. Kritsman writes: "After the Paris Commune, which created the first proletarian administration in the history of humanity, the next advance of principle was the development of a proletarian apparatus of economic management. This was achieved by the Russian revolution. . . . The Paris Commune created the *organisational form* for the political dictatorship of the proletariat, the Russian revolution that for its *economic dictatorship*. It is scarcely possible to overemphasise the importance of this achievement."[37] [My italics—*A.H.*]

The new formation was not designed in an exact fashion. At the time of the final drafting of *State and Revolution*, scarcely two months before the October revolution, Lenin considered the experience of the Paris Commune, or rather the markedly anti-bureaucratic marxist interpretation of it, as applicable to the whole of Soviet society—including the economy. (The greatness of Lenin lies not least in the fact that there was in him no trace of any attempt at self-justification.) The new form of administration developed (as is always the case, even today) in the course of social struggles within which ideologies, interests, needs, and the personal attributes of individuals acting in historical processes, were all inseparably welded together. What I shall try to show in the following pages can be no more than a few aspects of this many-sided "birth phase" which may help towards an understanding of the essence of this process.

The development of the Glavki

The first socialist system of economic administration developed in extraordinary circumstances in the course of the four years from 1918 to 1922. The world war, two revolutions and the civil war had totally disrupted the Russian economy. The following comparison given by Kritsman in 1924 in the *Vestnik Sotsialisticheskoi Akademii*[38] is indicative of the situation of industry:

Gross Product (in milliards of rubles)

Category	1913	1920	1920 production as a % of that of 1913
Heavy Industry	5620	1001	18%
Light Industry	1528	660	43%

At its nadir industrial production hardly reached 20% of the pre-war figure, and heavy industry suffered especially great damage.

It was no accident that it was precisely the sphere of industrial management where it became necessary in practice to institute an administrative apparatus separate from the direct producers which, given the necessary discipline and growth in professional knowledge, might relatively quickly master the difficulties. In the first years the economic situation only improved slowly. Nowadays it is difficult even to picture the Soviet Union of 1920 and 1921, for we must add to our picture of the devastated state of industry the catastrophic harvest of 1921, which struck the country at a point when the area under cultivation was already less than it had been before the war. On the one hand this situation led to terrible famine in 1921, and on the other it made the need for change obvious. The New Economic Policy opened up enormous possibilities for development, which justified not only NEP itself but also the economic institutions that had developed. What is more, it proved the necessity for the existence of the latter. We must realise that in a period of reconstruction during which industry is producing at twenty per cent of the pre-war level, even a fifty per cent rise in production would only mean that thirty per cent of the pre-war level had been achieved. Compared to many other countries in periods of reconstruction, a fifty per cent growth represents an exceptionally large upswing, and this seems to justify not only socialism in general but also the given form of the apparatuses running the economy. Almost like an avalanche, this strengthens the striving for centralisation.

Immediately after the October revolution, the management of industry was still performed by the Supreme Council of the National Economy (VSNKh), or its various vertically and horizontally organised departments, which worked like some sort of single giant state enterprise. However, this was only an initial stage. The most characteristic concrete form of the "economic dictatorship of the proletariat" was provided by the Glavki, or what in modern official jargon would be known as the Directorates of Industry. These worked under the direction of the Supreme Council of the National Economy and its local economic councils, and enjoyed substantially greater autonomy than the departments whose functions they had taken over. But in actual fact their development aided centralisation, which went with the growth in number of their tasks. This was because the economic system itself, into which these organisations fitted, remained unchanged until the introduction of the New Economic Policy.

No opposition of any significance arose against the idea of the unification of industry into a single organisation. The debate flowed around the functions of the Supreme Council of the National Economy and organisation which it built to carry them out. However, regardless of the debate, life itself demanded the establishment of an organisation of an industrial administration which was separate to some degree from central economic management, and in which representatives of trade unions and factory owners would take part, as well as delegates of the organs of central power.

During this period Lenin was very cautious in drawing up theoretical formulations. He preferred to try and get the feel of what was actually happening in practice. At the seventh Congress of the Russian Communist Party (Bolsheviks) in March 1918 he said, in opposition of Bukharin, "The bricks of which socialism will be composed have not yet been made. We cannot say anything further, and we should be as cautious and accurate as possible. . . . We are not in a position to give a description of socialism."[39] At the same time, if he did not have a definite point of view about the forms of economic system that could be successfully applied, Lenin did formulate the fundamental requirements. His first formulation appears in the article entitled "The Immediate Tasks of the Soviet Government".[40] In the same work he comes out against anarchism and anarcho-syndicalism as petty bourgeois tendencies, and demands the introduction of accounting and control in which the whole population would take part. It is worth noting that in Lenin's thought, the idea of "planning everything", which in a later debate with Trotsky he called a "technocratic illusion", does not occupy a prominent place. According to this way of thinking, with a few exceptions in the short period before War Communism, accounting and control was to take place in indices not of money but of kind. Monetary control was in any case impossible, since money was inflating rapidly and was disappearing almost completely from economic life.

Despite Lenin's wishes when he proclaimed the multiplicity of these forms and the impossibility of determining them in advance, we can already find in these concepts the germs of the kind of economic system which, when complete, might be called the "state administrative" type, based on planning methods operating mainly with indices in kind. However, in these years the system did not in practice develop into the complete form we knew later. We can consider War Communism as the first manifest form of the state administrative system; a primitive one, but perhaps its most pure form. For example, it was in these circumstances, and on the basis more of practical than of theoretical considerations, that the Executive Committee of the Paper Industry Directorate was set up with the following composition: a third from the trade union of the paper industry, a third from the central proletarian organisations, and a third from representatives of the Association of Industrialists. (A few months later the entrepreneurs were "expelled" from the Directorate.)

The most important function of these and other similar centres was that of control. They thus developed in the first instance as apparatuses of workers' control, concerned first of all with workers' control in the factory. The Centres and Directorates convened their own congresses and conferences, separate from those of the representatives of the various workers' organisations, and exercised real power over the administration that was now in the process of developing. If only because of this fact, we cannot consider these Directorates as developed bureaucratic institutions in the contemporary sociological sense.

At its outset "nationalisation" itself was, to a great extent, a movement from below. V. P. Milyutin has written that seventy per cent of the factories were nationalised because the decree on workers' control had not been implemented, or because the owner had fled, simply leaving the factory to its own fate. A small pamphlet of the time described this process in the following way: "When workers' control was introduced in a Siberian factory in Tobolsk district, the manager and the chief engineer went off to console the owner" and did not return. The factory remained without management and because of this the workers had to take it into their own hands. In the Uspenski factory (again in Tobolsk district) the owner went into hiding in January 1918, even before the introduction of workers' control, and the workers were obliged to take over the factory themselves. A great many such flights occurred.

The assault on the private ownership of the means of production in Soviet Russia began with the decree on workers' control, which can scarcely be considered to have been simply a tactical step. Rather, it embodied above all the concept that through the establishment of control the worker would achieve power over the capitalist owner, and over the capitalist factory management as well. The emphasis was not on the abstract property right, but on the real possibilities for the workers to handle decision-making. The claim for workers' control spread very quickly. It led to the complete abolition of private ownership, to the nationalisation first of large industry, then medium-sized and finally the most important small industries as well. In this process not only practical considerations (the flight of capitalists and capitalist managers) but ideological ones too (the creation of a unified national economy) played a role. Consequently the nationalisation of the means of production developed in such a way that the emphasis fell on a management from the ranks of the workers, and for a long time this appeared to be the only possible method. Here it is perhaps more difficult to assert that there was any other alternative. If we look at the practical situation, then we have to say that there hardly was. If, however, we consider the question at a theoretical level, then without a doubt a possible solution existed in which the emphasis would have fallen on the realisation of workers' control and not on the creation of a new administration by means of the promotion of some workers. The problems of Soviet reality, however, made the latter solution imperative.

In June 1918, the Council of People's Commissars promulgated the decree on the nationalisation of the larger factories, and with this was born the need to integrate the branches of the economy. This increased both the power and the number of the Glavki and different types of Centres. At the same time it necessitated changes in the methods of management. Because of the campaign-like nature of the nationalisation programme, the first period was characterised by decentralisation. But in fact the establishment of this organisational form of nationalisation was strengthened and mutually supported by the taking of large industrial plants into state ownership (which completely took over the tasks of accounting and control), and by the increasing emphasis placed on centralisation and the administration. Thus in the years 1918-19 the system of "Glavkism" was greatly consolidated. Large apparatuses came into existence, and scarcely two years after the victory of the revolution they were already coming to constitute a bureaucratic system of their own.

Despite all its negative aspects "Glavkism" conformed to the objective historical need, and in this respect it was perhaps the most adequate form of economic management for "War Communism". This is not contradicted by the fact that it provoked trenchant opposition which developed with extraordinary speed into a critique of Glavkism as a bureaucratic distortion of socialism. Such opposition only increased as more emphasis was placed on the administration.

In the first period the Centres and Directorates of industry had a clearly social character. They were organised under corporate leadership, as can be seen from the composition of the Paper

Industry Directorate. This type of leadership did not last for long. An important part was played in its eclipse by the ideology of centralism and one-man management, which had developed under the pressure of historical circumstances and which now became prevalent largely as a reaction to the strengthened anarchist tendencies of 1918.

From the point of view of its formal traits, the developing administration of socialist society corresponded more and more to those criteria which characterise a bureaucracy in the sociological sense of the word: that is to say, those who work within it fulfil their tasks as a vocation, as their principal occupation, and with an ever-growing degree of separation. The difference between the types of administration that develop alongside private property and those that develop in societies which are abolishing private property is a different question, and I do not consider it the task of this essay to discuss it in detail, more especially since I have dealt with it in other studies. The development within socialist society of an administrative management with the formal traits of bureaucracy subsequently became inseparably bound up with the centralised economic system, based on the fulfilment of planning directives. Alongside the tasks of accounting and control which had developed earlier, the operation of central planning justified the establishment of administrative apparatuses having huge powers at their disposal, while on the other hand it to a large extent limited their concrete organisational form, as well as the internal structure of the individual apparatuses. For example, the hegemony of those apparatuses which dealt with planning directives and the supervision of plans became almost general.

In the early years the Glavki, even at their most developed, were simply the directing agencies of production within the state administration, and not independent economic organs. They were called upon to make a "breakdown" of the production plans which they received from the Supreme Council of the National Economy, and to supervise their fulfilment. In theory they were supposed to hand the whole of their production over to the Directorates which dealt with distribution. In practice, of course, they could not do this, and so they disposed of a part of their production themselves, by the direct exchange of products. However, at the time of War Communism this was considered a kind of distortion, a relic surviving from capitalism.

Though the necessity for the establishment of the Glavki was generally recognised, the question of how they were viewed, and by whom, is a valid one. Yuri Larin, for example, considered that

132

these institutions corresponded completely to the socialist nature of management, that they were socialist organisations *par excellence*. For those who thought like him, any attempt to surpass them could only be a step backwards. Others, however, saw in this management system a form characteristic of state capitalism. Such people either searched feverishly for some other sort of solution which would correspond more to socialist principles, or they accepted it as a practical necessity. Besides these extreme viewpoints, there also appeared another point of view which today we might perhaps call a historical, structural analysis. For example, M. Sovelev wrote about the Glavki that, "precisely because of their so-called bureaucratic and non-socialist character, they played a colossal role as forms of industrial organisation that served to incorporate the productive workers into a unified production apparatus."[41]

As I have already said, the Glavki were the adequate institutional forms for the management of industry, and indeed for the economy as a whole, under War Communism. As the preconditions for surpassing War Communism arrived, so the outlines of new managerial forms unfolded. These mainly found expression in the trust institutions which were seen as successors to the Glavki. However, before I attempt to describe these new institutions, I must return to the former institutions themselves for an understanding of the real situation.

War Communism was naturally a much more complex phenomenon than the idea of it that lives in the consciousness of today's university students. It was characterised not only by the striving for centralism, but by decentralising tendencies as well. These arose inevitably from the campaign-like nature of nationalisation, and also from the particular way of thinking represented chiefly by Lenin. He proclaimed a freedom of forms, because he wanted thus to make it easier for the initiative of the masses to be expressed. Besides this, the external and internal conditions necessary for centralisation had not yet arisen. The system of compulsory agricultural deliveries to the state was not designed to end the system of material incentives, as it is often interpreted today. On the contrary, in the given circumstances it was the only possible means of *providing* incentives, in a country ravaged by inflation and with its industry in ruins. Its true aim was to create incentives for the workers, even if this was to be achieved mostly at the expense of the interests of the peasants.

I wish to show by all this that NEP was not a homogeneous negation of War Communism as some kind of "distilled" system,

133

but rather its transcendence, a step forward in the true meaning of the term. Of course it was not free from contradiction, not even as a pure ideal type (and least of all in its practical realisation). It was, rather, a step which succeeded as a result of social struggle. It was not the only possibility, but the victorious alternative in a concrete historical situation. While NEP on the one hand abolished Glavkism, on the other hand it strengthened its supervision over the economic units, which were changing from institutions directly financed and controlled by the state budget into self-accounting ones. It even prepared for their incorporation into the unified plan system. Smilga was justified in saying that "in such approximations, it must be recognised that our trusts are *social joint-stock companies* in which a hundred per cent of the shares are held by the state." [My emphasis—*A.H.*] In opposition to ideological arguments that the introduction of NEP had betrayed the achievements of the October revolution, he states: "We can only smile at these worries. We stress that in our opinion there is nothing new in principle. We only want to strengthen what has already objectively become fact."[42]

The New Economic Policy and the formation of the trusts

Economic reforms are always the results of a joint application of the attitudes of *Sein*, what is given, and *Sollen*, what ought to be, and as such they necessarily integrate both fact and value orientations. They must take into consideration what is new and developing, give ideological and practical support to it, and condemn those institutions and management forms which have been superseded in practice, so as to make them disappear more rapidly. Both tasks simultaneously require an exceptionally careful analysis of the given situation and, on the basis of a very carefully considered value system, the choice of the most auspicious solution from among the possible alternatives.

At the time of the introduction of the New Economic Policy the Soviet leaders carried out such a necessary analysis, and this enabled a wide-ranging debate to take place over the chosen values. Lenin did not simply assert that the new situation demanded a new policy. He resolutely declared that the party had made an error when it had delayed the preparation of reforms. This assertion did not meet with general approval at the time. Many tried to argue that this "mistake" was a historical necessity. "In general," wrote Radek, "our earlier policy was in no way a mistake, and it is due to the fact that we carried it through with iron consistency that we vanquished the internal and external opposition and created the preconditions for the present policy."[43] The question of whether the New Economic Policy was an enforced step backwards or an organisational consequence of the October revolution, an alternative economic system which enriched socialism with new elements, is still urgently debated today. S. Gusev resolutely declared that "but for the civil war, we would have introduced essentially the same economic policy as early as 1919-1920, and not the policy of War Communism which was forced upon us by the war. We would have carried out nationalisation carefully, restricting it to large factories on which we would have wanted to concentrate all our strength."[44]

One of the most important organisational changes brought in by NEP was that the Glavki and the main Directorates, which reflected and represented strong centralising tendencies, were superseded by the trusts. According to the original conception of trusts, they were only intended to serve the functions of administration (supervision and co-ordination) while the previously centralised economic tasks were transferred to the factories. According to this conception, since the factories acquired a relatively large degree of autonomy, and since they assumed a commercial nature on the basis of the relations between them, "the supervision and regulation of the work of the factories, that is of the degree of competition or co-operation between them, become of exceptionally great importance."[45] So, as we can see from this view, centralised economic direction is in no way negated. Rather, it is reconciled with the relative independence of the enterprises, and at the same time it develops an ideological foundation.

Ideas arose to the effect that the setting up of trusts, which had gained in strength under NEP and won legal recognition, led to these economic institutions being completely separated from the state, that is from the institutions of the Supreme Council of the National Economy, and thus to the transformation of the latter into an old-style ministry. Smilga answered these "worries" in *Narodnoe khozyaïstvo*, saying that "no such process is taking place. The fact that the state is the proprietor of heavy industry excludes such possibilities. It does not allow either the complete self-administration of industry, or a return to the old ministerial style. The normative-regulatory task of the old ministry of commercial and industrial affairs does not correspond in any way to the economic functions of the Supreme Council of the National Economy."[46]

When Smilga wrote these lines the trusts which had "split away" from the central state administration were already beginning to be brought back under the direction of the Supreme Council of the National Economy. According to Smilga one of the biggest mistakes of Glavkism was that the "Directorates" had combined both strategic and tactical tasks, whereas with the implementation of NEP they were entrusted, in theory at least, to two separate organs. The strategic tasks were given to the Supreme Council of the National Economy, the tactical ones to the trusts.

The setting up of trusts, which it is usual to consider as superseding the institutions of Glavkism, was gaining strength in the formal sense by 1920, but at that time their content was essentially somewhat different. For example, in *Narodnoe khozaïstvo* in 1920 we can already read an account of the results of setting up trusts, and we can also find fairly precise details about the course it took: "The setting up of trusts nominally acknowledges the autonomy of every individual enterprise; in practice however it restricts it, destroying its unique existence, and transforms each given enterprise into a subsidiary section of one big, gigantic trust."[47] Incidentally, in the rest of his article, the writer further justifies our earlier assertion that, in comparison with the Glavki which at their inception worked as loose syndicates, the trusts (before NEP) were conceived as economic institutions working according to a "single plan" and with a "single budget".

The transition from Glavkism to trusts did not always signify a radical change because, after all, a section of the Glavki had already become trusts under the pressure of natural constraints, before this had been recognised either in law or in economic policy. Nevertheless, to public opinion they appeared as the typical organisational forms of two differing economic systems. The Glavki appeared to represent the "state administrative" system, the trusts the system based on "self-accounting".* I consider the latter system to be a new and essentially different type of economic system when compared to the state administrative type. In the pure form of this system, the reduction of production costs, the achievement of profits by the enterprises, prices based on production costs, or volume indices calculated on this basis, are all used as the chief indices of direct management.

The trusts of War Communism naturally differed from those of NEP. The difference lies primarily in the fact that the latter were

---

* The distinction between the various types of socialist economic system is explained more fully in the next essay.

self-accounting units while the former, to use our modern jargon, were state-financed institutions, if we can use such an expression at all when talking of an economic form which developed in Soviet industry in 1918-19, and which was merely the herald of the "state administrative" economic system rather than its actual fore-bear. The War Communism trusts, if they were ever called that (even the change in the use of the word is interesting) functioned in a completely different way from those of NEP. We, who in our socialist practice use either expression quite naturally without thinking to distinguish between them, do not immediately realise that in the Soviet Union at the beginning of the twenties the contexts in which they appeared had entirely different associations. The Directorate or Glavok was an inheritance from the tsarist étatist bureaucracy. The trust was imported from the capitalist economy, which the new system in its first phase had wanted to negate in every respect. By 1922, in any case, a wide-ranging debate had broken out in the Soviet Union about the nature of the trusts, and in the course of this debate opinions were even formulated to the effect that the trusts should develop into enterprises working with fully independent responsibility: almost, one might say, socialist business ventures. (This may not be exactly the expression we would use today, but I think it represents the essence of the matter.)*

But according to the prevalent and official point of view, the nature of the trusts can be summarised, albeit with some simpli-fication, in the following sociological characterisation: (a) The trust is similar to a joint-stock company in which the majority of shares are held by the state; (b) the trust operates on the basis of commercial methods and market forces with the aim of making a profit; (c) the trust functions on the basis of self-accounting (the *khozraschot* principle), which originally meant that the right to the appropriation of a part of the surplus product was recognised; (d) the state, as sole shareholder, has the right to supervise the nomination of the management of the trust and its activities, and this is done in the name of the state by the Supreme Council of the National Economy, or by the economic organs under its direction.

One of the essential aspects of War Communism was the central distribution of products, not in terms of money but in kind and in their specific material units. This was also one of the main func-

---

* Elsewhere in the text the expression "socialist enterprise" is used in this context (*trans.*).

tions of the Glavki. The new system brought in by NEP put more emphasis on the recognition of market forces; the trusts, operating as independent economic institutions, had to realise the results of their activities mainly in monetary indices. The principle of centralised accounting in kind was thus replaced by the system of self-accounting, which expresses the results in monetary terms. However, at the time of the introduction of NEP, the practical realisation of the independence of the trusts was hindered by many things. Even at the outset, in contradiction to the idea that every product should be put on the market and that the state as consumer should be on a par with all other consumers (Osinski formulated this requirement very precisely), many products came under central distribution. Thus the return to the state administrative system actually began even before any radical break with the principle of the self-accounting system had occurred.

NEP also introduced administrative or official prices, which were formed on the basis of ideological rather than economic considerations. This strengthened Glavkism rather than the basic ideas of NEP, and thus centralised accounting was retained, even in the self-accounting system. The principle of centralised accounting did not lose its viability even in the era of NEP, having already been formulated at the time of War Communism.

Those revolutionaries who had some economic knowledge, first and foremost Lenin, almost immediately sensed that centralised accounting was of incomparably greater importance in the new order than it had been under capitalism. NEP developed this further into the principle of self-accounting, by which its importance is, however, in no way belittled. The economic system based on the exchange of material units, which prevailed from 1918 to 1920, made centralised accounting necessary. However, when the change-over to production for the market began in 1921, this brought with it the self-accounting principle, though without involving any really essential change. Success was still not judged on market principles, but on calculations made by the higher organs of the administration.

Centralised accounting demanded the construction of large central supervisory apparatuses, just as the principle of self-accounting does. Institutions with functions similar to the old capitalist state supervision are unsuited to this task from two points of view. They are too obsessed with the problems of the national budget, and they exclude the masses. In his much discussed book on the economics of the transition period, Bukharin stated that the old capitalist forms of accounting had become obsolete, and that in the new situation it was necessary to go over to centralised accounting with indices in kind. Chayanov reached a similar conclusion. He wanted to construct a natural unit that would be applicable to every product and that would make it possible to dispense with money. The attempt to provide a self-justifying ideology for the state administrative economy, can already be discerned in these views. One manifestation of this was the view that expended labour could serve as a direct measure of value without the mediation of money.

The development of the power structure of the socialist state.

At the end of 1919 the Soviet state had consolidated itself militarily, but in the field of production it was faced with unprecedented difficulties, which appeared almost insurmountable. The greater part of the peasantry wanted to produce for their own needs alone. A large part of the workers had abandoned the famine-stricken towns. In this exceptionally difficult economic situation the questions that were formulated were firstly ones of the "how can things go on?" type.

Socialism is characterised by the contradiction that it simultaneously requires both the construction of a developed administration which will have interests of its own, and control by society of any such administration. Thus within a few months, two clearly contradictory trends emerged.

On one side stood Trotsky, the commander-in-chief of the victorious Red Army who, on the basis of his wartime experiences, wanted to reorganise production under the direction of an essentially military command with strict one-man management. In the construction of a unified and monolithic power structure he saw structure the best guarantee for strengthening the revolutionary achievements. "Bureaucracy," he said "was not invented by tsarism. It has existed throughout a great period in the development of humanity, a period which has in no way come to an end." He came out for the strengthening of the administration at all costs, including the privileges to be given to the administration. As his biographer Isaac Deutscher says of him, he thus became the spokesman of the administrative group.[48] The position he adopted in the trade union debate followed directly from this standpoint. His view was that the trade unions should be incorporated into the order of state administration: the trade-union leaders' task was to strengthen labour discipline and to raise production.

On the other side stood the "Workers' Opposition" and the "Decists" (the group of "Democratic Centralists") who, drawing their support mainly from the trade unions, demanded a "producers' democracy" in opposition to one-man management and the hierarchically structured administration. Their demands were built around the idea, central to the trade unions, that the organs of economic management at every level should be elected through the trade unions, in order that they should directly represent the workers, or at least their trade unions. Besides this, the ideas of the Workers' Opposition were full of the most romantic of communist illusions (free food supplies, free clothing and free housing for the workers). Their conceptions were not very far removed from the economic programme of the anarchists, according to whom the factories had to be transformed into production co-operatives and given over to the immediate producers, to collectives which would enter into unregulated exchange relations with each other. According to them, the communist principle of supply "from each according to his abilities, to each according to his needs" could be realised without any transition period. This alternative is the practical formulation of the historical idea represented chiefly by Fourier, Proudhon and Sorel. This similarity was clearly sensed by the economist Tugan-Baranovsky, who explained why the anarchists considered co-operative property to be a more advanced form than state property: "In a co-operative there is no oppressive power, there is no rule of the majority over the minority as there is in socialism. The co-operative ideal coincides with the ideal of modern anarchism."[49]

Lenin's role at this time can scarcely be overestimated, for he did not accept that these solutions were "either/or" alternatives. Soviet society, in no small measure under Lenin's personal influence, thus embarked in these years on a path which retained the rational core of both standpoints, without adopting their extremes. This was not the behaviour of "a genius for compromise" (the expression is Lunacharsky's), but rather that of a man who had an inspired grasp of the situation and could perhaps sense the alternatives of development that had become possible, and could choose between them on the basis of an unshakeable value commitment.

Lenin's theoretical works on the economic system of socialism (I am thinking here mainly of his writings on NEP), and on the character of state power, managed to reflect almost every problem of the new socio-economic formation of socialism without ever becoming a closed theory. To put it in another way, his ideas did not become *the* theory of socialism in the sense that the theory of classical European capitalism can be found in Marx's *Capital*. The big difference between their two situations is that the social order which Marx theorised had already ripened to the point where its "self-analysis" was possible, whereas the socialism of Lenin's time lived much more in the world of conceptions about different alternatives of development than in the actual world of social reality.

In my opinion, the most important of the concepts expressed by Lenin about the administration of the new society, or at least the most important of those supported by him, was "Soviet taylorism" and the principle of one-man management. Lenin recognised that "all administrative work requires special qualifications. . . . A knowledge of all the conditions of production down to the last detail and of the latest technology of your branch of production is required: you must have had a certain scientific training. . . . We are not opposed to placing workers at the head, but we say that this question must be settled in the interests of production."[50] This question is linked with the need to popularise taylorism, which Lenin accepted. He set out from the standpoint that "we, the party of the proletariat, have no other way of acquiring the ability to organise large-scale production on trust lines, as trusts are organised, except by acquiring it from first-class capitalist experts."[51]

In this period, the weakness in specialised administrative knowledge led to such chronic problems that the blame for almost every negative character of management, including bureaucracy, was inevitably heaped on it. As Krupskaya put it: "The root of bureaucracy does not lie in the malevolence of this or that group of individuals, but in the absence of knowledge of the planned, rational organisation of work. The matter of administration is in no way a simple one."[52] In the same article we can read the following remarks about Taylor: "We can learn a very great deal from Taylor. Though he dealt above all with the situation of the factory worker, we can and must use in our work a lot of the organisational principles he suggests."

NEP raised the need for good businessmen to be placed boldly in the posts of "red directors". This demand was no smaller than that which our Hungarian new economic system asks in its selection of economic managers, but the demand of those days reflected a less developed stage. Not many years later the businessmen were followed by directors recruited from among "good technicians", and it is only nowadays that we have reached the need for a type

141

of director whom we can call "the socialist manager".

When it came to solving the cadre question in the Soviet Union the old experts were hardly relied on at all, if only because there were very few of them, and even fewer were left after the revolution and civil war. A report presented to the Eighth Congress of Soviets by the Supreme Council of the National Economy provides some interesting figures on the formation of the Soviet economic apparatus:

Representative sample of the permanent staff of the
Soviet economic management apparatus in 1920[53]

Management Organ	Total	Workers	Experts	Officials
National and provincial councils of the national economy	187	107 (57%)	22 (12%)	58 (31%)
Directorates (Glavki)	184	48 (26%)	72 (39%)	64 (35%)
Factory management	1143	726 (63%)	398 (35%)	19 (2%)
	1514	881 (58%)	492 (33%)	141 (9%)

The most interesting fact for us in this data is that it was precisely the Glavki which employed the most experts.

The following case is characteristic of the situation that existed at that time. In the summer of 1922, 270 engineers who worked in Moscow's trusts and other institutions were asked to complete a questionnaire. The results were published in *Pravda* (no. 127). Those who answered were divided into two groups. Those in the first group had taken part in the hierarchy of economic management before the revolution. Those in the second had not. Among other things they were asked whether they sympathised with Soviet power. In the first group, nine per cent answered "Yes", and in the second group, thirteen per cent answered "Yes". When asked whether they considered their work useful, thirty per cent in the first group and seventy-five per cent in the second answered "Yes".

In this situation it is easy to understand Lenin's point of view. He placed the emphasis on study, on the education of new economic managers, and where taylorism is concerned he formulated the following task, which is still appropriate even today: "Our primary and most important task is to . . . adopt everything that is truly valuable in European and American science."[54] This question of recognising the importance of special administrative knowledge is essentially linked with Lenin's support for one-man management of economic enterprises as opposed to corporate

142

management. Again, we must understand this as a pragmatic alternative in the relations of the given period, and not as some sort of general law of socialism. He formulated the need for one-man management precisely when the victory of the Soviet state over foreign intervention had been assured, and when Trotsky had already elaborated his own theory for the military organisation of production.

"Corporate management," writes Lenin, "as the chief type of organisation of Soviet administration, is something embryonic, something needed in the early stages when you have to start from scratch. But when more or less stable forms have been established, the transition to practical work involves individual management, for that system best ensures the most effective utilisation of human abilities, and a real, not verbal, verification of work done. . . . And taking the experience of the army, we find in the organisation of its administration a systematic development from the original forms, from the corporate principle to the individual principle."[55] The demand for corporate management was the demand of the Workers' Opposition which, as Lenin remarked at the Ninth Congress, was saturated with hatred for experts and lack of knowledge.

The economic system based on self-accounting, in the development of which Lenin's creative genius had played an important role, had scarcely been put into practice by the end of the twenties. A peculiar collusion of circumstances then led to a return of the "state administrative" economic system, even though it was at a higher level. Nowadays, however, we can witness simultaneous attempts both to create a more consistent kind of self-accounting system and to develop a new type of socialist economic system in which the firm is no longer just a self-accounting unit but an independent socialist enterprise. Here, production prices are not decided administratively but on the open market, or at least it is market forces that play the leading role; as a result, the socialist planned economy is realised by indirect managerial methods.

The alternative types of socialist economic system that have thus developed—the state administrative type, the self-accounting type, and socialist enterprise—are not strictly antagonistic forms. They can all serve as creative elements in a rationally constructed economy. There will be branches of the national economy where it is appropriate to adopt an economic system of the state administrative type, others where the self-accounting system is applicable, and yet others where socialist enterprise is the most suitable.

143

IX: Economic Reform and the Basic Types of Socialist Economic System

The "micro-sociological" school is a widespread one in sociology. Like micro-economics, it does not study the enterprise in general nor bureaucratic phenomena in their broader social and economic interrelations; the sociological approach in the marxist sense is therefore necessarily driven into the background, and what come to the fore are the psychological factors peculiar to the "socio-technical" school and to other social research approaches such as those based on factory organisation, industrial economics, etc. These trends are today being criticised not only by marxists but also by various bourgeois circles, who are trying to get beyond them. It is no exaggeration to state that phenomena within enterprises and thus also the relations between the various management and control bodies, if they really are of a sociological nature, remain incomprehensible if we do not take into consideration the socio-economic macrostructure in which the given enterprise operates, and this macrostructure embraces the economy itself. A sociological analysis of the real functioning of central economic management and control is likewise impossible without an understanding of the macrostructure, which primarily means the functioning of the specific economic régimes and their effects on economic life. I should like here to emphasise just one aspect of this extremely complex set of topics. I shall try to analyse specific economies by way of the basic systems within them, and by way of the economic subsystems (financing, the labour and wages subsystem, etc.) and institutions, and the vertical and horizontal relationships between them, which together form a consistent unity.

The necessary heterogeneity of the economy, and the basic types of economic system

Economic thinking still tends to visualise a specific economic system as some kind of homogeneous type ruled by uniform principles and methods of control, or where this is not yet the case it is assumed that this type must be helped into existence. If we compare the economic systems which have developed under socialist relations from the standpoint of their characteristic types of management and control, then we shall find three basic types, which appear in various "amalgams" in the economies of various eras.

(1) "Natural" administrative management. Here the goals of the individual enterprise, together with the means utilised to attain these goals, are determined not by money but by material indices. The basic principle of this management system is planning, stock-taking and distribution *in kind*. This means that the institutions and enterprises involved operate with a minimum of autonomy, as organisational units of a national economy which is itself envisaged as a single enterprise.

(2) The *khozraschot*, which we shall call the "self-accounting system". The important special feature of this is that, in comparison with the first type, the role of money increases at the expense of material indices. In this system, the main goals of enterprise management take the form of various indices expressed in money terms, such as the value of the gross product, the value of the per capita product, or the rate or sum of enterprise profit. One or another of these indices takes priority in different periods, but they have a common problem, which stems from the fact that they are based on a pricing system for goods and services that is formed not by economic life but by the decision-making processes which take place in the various special organs of control (I shall call them "administrative prices"), and is invariably founded on the "weighted" balancing of *ex-ante* and *ex-post* cost accounts. In other words, even in the most varied forms of this system, the essence of price formation is that the state covers the investment costs of producing those goods or performing those services which it considers necessary, i.e. it stipulates them in the plans, and the relevant administrative organs ratify them. At the same time, enterprise profits are built into prices as a predetermined percentage. This means, in fact, that in an economic system which is based on enterprises operating as self-accounting units, each enterprise works at a profit *in practice* as well as *in principle,* and losses occur only rarely. This, of course, reduces the various kinds of profit index to a complete fiction, just as it does the indices of gross production and of productivity. In this system, the main aim is to raise living standards by reducing production costs and prices. (There is another question which deserves separate analysis. How has this phenomenon distorted and how does it continue to distort the calculation of growth in national income, and what part has this played in forming the opinion that the progress of the socialist

145

countries is dynamic enough not to need modifications in their economic management systems?).

(3) Socialist enterprise. This differs from the second type in that the prices of its goods and services depend on economic and market relations, and not on whether some authority justifies the prices reached on the basis of investments and profits calculated *ex-ante* and *ex-post*. In this system it stands to reason that there can and must be enterprises operating at a deficit, that is to say, enterprises incapable of producing at a technical and organisational level advanced enough to enable them to operate below the marginal costs which have developed in the course of competition. Under this economic system, the main aim is to develop a model of production according to which, by means of the labour power available, the highest use-value and exchange-value can be produced.

How the various basic types have become predominent in different historical eras

The three basic types of economic control system outlined here did not follow each other in historical sequence, nor did they assume a predominant role by replacing each other. The first kind, the "natural", "administrative" management system, developed first in the Soviet Union. The historical and economic situation which followed the October revolution practically demanded the introduction of an all-embracing centralised system, in which money did not play an important role either in accounting or in control. This necessity appeared in the form of "natural" administrative management and the control system of war communism.

The outlines of the *khozraschot,* the self-accounting system, developed while the New Economic Policy (NEP) was being worked out. Compared to the preceding stage, it secured an incomparably greater degree of independence for enterprises, while promising a changeover to planning, accounting and distribution in money terms. But within a very short time, before the principles of an economic system based on self-accounting could be introduced in practice, this specific economic system became rigid and in many ways returned to the principles of the previous one. An analysis of the question of whether this return was necessary would take us far out of our way. In my opinion, it can be considered as no more than *one alternative* of development; it became predominant in a given historical situation and as the result of a struggle between various social forces, but it was by no means the only road that could have been followed.

The "natural" administrative management system was, in essence, introduced in Hungary in the early 1950s, or rather this was the system that gained the predominant role in Hungary's economy. The principle of self-accounting was asserted in various statements, but not in practice. This can be easily proved by studying any of the economic subsystems which we have referred to. The changes which took place in the management system after 1956 can be called a genuine advance of the principle of self-accounting into the sphere of practice. The attempts at reform which can be observed at present in the Soviet Union (the most radical representative of which is perhaps Professor Liberman) and in the German Democratic Republic can, in fact, also be considered as simply a return to the economic system based on self-accounting which was prefigured in Lenin's NEP. This system retains the method of control by means of instructions stipulated in planning, but it contains a radical reduction in the number of indices and increases the number of indices expressed in money at the expense of those expressed in material units, though the "administrative" nature of the pricing system is left unchanged. Under this system, the independence of enterprises can be substantially extended, but they cannot develop from "self-accounting units" into "independent socialist enterprises".

Hungary undertook a large-scale experiment going beyond this position, working out the principles of a new system of economic control and management, and beginning to implement it. No matter how important we regard the decision to implement the economic reform, however, we should not make the mistake of imagining the institutional structure of economic life to be some kind of homogeneous, monolithic system. We should recognise the fact that we can find sectors (industrial branches, trading functions, etc.) in which the "natural" "administrative" management system is best, some in which self-accounting is best, and others in which the principles of the new management system, the creation of socialist enterprise, is best suited to our aims. Depending on the peculiarities of individual spheres, the solutions which ensure the greatest effectiveness may vary in each of them. This means that the development of the economy in the socialist societies of today is confronted not so much with a choice between two alternatives but rather (and particularly when the higher level of economic development is taken into consideration) with the search for a simultaneous and joint application of various economic systems, for an optimum choice of the system 'most suited so far to the peculiarities of individual economic spheres, a choice from among the principles and methods of the economic systems which have developed historically. For this reason, it is not always the same basic type from among those listed above that will play the predominant role.

But as far as social consciousness or even economic thinking are concerned, we have still not got past the stage of talking about "pure economic régimes" or about the impossibility of the fact that management methods, institutional structures, decision-making and information systems can and must be formed in accordance with the peculiarities of the branches concerned. (Behind this concept of "homogenising" the economy we can also find the concept of socialist property relations as a homogeneous, monolithic whole. I have criticised this concept and analysed the various forms of socialist property in the essay on property relations.)

If we interpret economic systems in the way that I have suggested, it places the debate about centralism (which is very often treated as a choice between two alternatives) in a completely different light. The economic systems as outlined above essentially posit the field of motion for centralisation and decentralisation, though obviously they do not determine them unequivocally. This is why I cannot accept the widespread view that the essence of the economic reforms which have taken place in the European socialist countries is decentralisation. This view was stated recently by two left-wing West German economists. Altvater and Neusüss, when they wrote: "The basic principle of the economic reforms is that if the bureaucracy is forced to acknowledge the inefficiency of its own centralised form, it decentralises itself. This decentralisation is the essence of the economic reforms." In my opinion, neither centralisation nor decentralisation are part of the essence of the economic reforms; they are simply phenomena which accompany varied and substantial changes, of which one of the most important fields of motion is a change in the role of the three basic types within the framework of a single economy. If we take this approach, then one of the most essential features of the new management system is by no means decentralisation but the fact that in many fields of economic life, economic bodies of the "socialist enterprise" type are being set up in place of administratively controlled institutions, or else in place of (or alongside) enterprises which operate as self-accounting units. This changes the entire substance of the structure.

It is natural, of course (and this is why I used the word "along-side" in the penultimate sentence), that this management principle cannot be given a predominant role in every sphere of economic life. There are two main reasons why this cannot be done. First of all, there are and always will be spheres of economic life whose functions, for structural reasons, would be better served by maintaining or setting up administratively controlled institutions and enterprises operating as self-accounting units (e.g. the war industry, electricity, railways, to name only the obvious examples). The second reason is that there are a number of comparatively important branches of the economic and industrial structure which were developed under the old economic system and where, if the "socialist enterprise" principle were introduced, tremendous difficulties would arise for the functioning of that particular branch, creating a substantial drop in domestic production; this would cause an intolerable economic and social shock not only to that particular branch but to society as a whole. (I consider mining and metallurgy to be such branches.)

By way of a digressive and perhaps grotesque analogy, I would like to point out that the appearance of the "natural", "administrative" type and of the "self-accounting" type can be clearly observed in the development of the modern capitalist economy too. The former can be found in the form of capitalist government ownership, and the latter in the form of multinational companies. If I were not against being thought to adhere to mechanistic and determinist "convergence" theories which I myself have criticised, I would say that while the capitalist enterprise system is being complemented by these two forms, in the socialist countries these same two forms (which have ruled alone until now) are being complemented by "socialist enterprise". However, this analogy is an oversimplification, and fails to take account of some very important aspects of social life: the former instance essentially retains the bourgeois system of private ownership, while the latter does away with it completely.

From what I have said so far, it becomes quite clear that the economies which have developed in the European socialist societies contain all three types. (This assumes that they are all experiencing healthy progress. Those socialist countries where primitive accumulation and an enforced limitation on basic necessities still exists raise a completely different problem, and thus my conclusions do not refer to them.) The main question, therefore, is as follows: which of the various economic methods and institutional types should be given priority *in various branches* and *at*

149

various historical periods, and which of them should be given a predominant role, given the peculiarities of the different branches? It seems to me that conscious heterogeneity within the economy would thus be a victory for rationality over attempts at homogenisation which in any case were originally ideological in character and today seem irrational. If our point of departure is the heterogeneity which appears within one economy, then the three types of system listed at the beginning of this essay may only be distinguished from each other as analytic categories; in practice, they appear jointly (though with different emphasis) within the economies of the individual countries. The nature of this "amalgam" is influenced not only by the struggles of social forces with differing interests but also by a number of objective factors (the importance of foreign trade, the role of war production, etc.).

The basic types of economic system and the institutional system

From a social point of view, the three basic types of economic system demand very different types of control organ, even at the highest level of management, i.e. the ministerial level. When the first type is dominant, the control organs are stamped with the seal of governmental administration, and a particularly big role is given to planning bodies and to various budgeting and supervisory departments. The emphasis, as I have said, is on planning, accounting and distributing absolutely everything, and this requires the creation of an inflated central apparatus. The various organs form a hierarchical order, with the central planning office at the summit. When the second type is dominant, the economic ministries take on an "industrial management" character. Alongside the appearance of money indices, various types of financial management and control organs come to the forefront, substantially increasing the role of central pricing, price control bodies and the accounting sections of the ministries. Within the hierarchy of central economic management organs, the central planning office and the ministry of finance share first place. When the third type is dominant, the "industrial management" character of ministerial organs disappears, and gradually the ministries are no longer responsible for the enterprises under their supervision but only for the main development guidelines of the various branches. This means that the economic ministries are increasingly involved in economic *policy,* and their actual administrative activities are achieved mainly by indirect methods. There is a kind of division of labour, in which the rivalry between the central planning office and the ministry of finance disappears, since the former gradually reduces its interference in the everyday practice of economic management (this role is handed over to the financial management bodies) and its activities in long-term planning become central.

The change is perhaps even greater (and more easily recognisable in practice) in the social character of enterprise management. In the first type, the head of the enterprise or institute is, in fact, the number one government official (this was Stalin's definition). In the second type, technical and economic tasks form a stronger part of enterprise management, and thus under this system the technical and economic skills of enterprise managers receive increased emphasis. In the third type, however, socialist enterprise needs managers who, along with their technical and economic knowledge (and often even at the cost of this) must have a broad knowledge of the market, together with co-ordinating skills and experience of the highest order; they must be able and unafraid to make definite decisions, even in cases where serious risks have to be taken: this type of manager is in keeping with the ideal image that is drawn of the socialist manager.

As far as institutions are concerned, there is another important change that needs to be noted, which has a tremendous effect on economic life. This is the different and changed character of the direct economic ties between institutions. The "natural", "administrative" system of management is dominated by vertical ties, while in socialist enterprise the dominant form is that of horizontal ties; here too, the "self-accounting" system lies somewhere between the two extremes.

Changes in the subsystems of the basic economic systems

The three basic economic systems outlined here, primarily for analytic purposes, naturally determine the major features of the economic and economic control subsystems operating within them. For functionally specialised management, whose job includes the creation of economic subsystems, a careful study of these is particularly important. But the working methods of central control and management bodies differ substantially from each other, depending on which of the economic systems plays a dominant role in the given field, or which system can usefully be applied. In order to demonstrate this, I shall provide a very sketchy (and therefore, no doubt, very exaggerated) review of the changes in

151

the sphere of activities of just three functional subsystems: planning, financial management, and labour management (or the field of labour in the broader sense).

(1) In the "administrative" management system, *planning* extends its attention to everything. This is marked to a great extent by its attempt to calculate everything in material units; the emphasis is much more on the accurate fulfilment of directives for distribution and production, than on foreseeing opportunities, or on making an expert choice of the means necessary for setting and meeting goals. Even if longer-term goals exist, they are determined far more by political and ideological motives than by economic calculations. Money, and indices based on prices, play a comparatively small role. A natural concomitant of this system, if it becomes predominant, is the striving for self-sufficiency; the tacit aim of this is to satisfy calculated needs as far as possible through domestic production, which means that planning also strives for an autarkic physical balance.

The introduction of the self-accounting principle (that is, if it really is introduced, not simply announced) relieves planning of a number of detail jobs; instead, questions of perspective, and together with this the criterion of economic efficiency, come to the fore. In this system, money begins to play its own role in economic management; but its function is still very restricted, for all indices expressed in money terms are tied to producer and service prices, which are determined by administrative organs—and this means that the decisions of administrative management dominate the economic factors. (By saying this, I certainly do not mean to deny that in some cases administrative prices can approximate to economic or market prices; but the essential features of the system prevent this from becoming prevalent.) Thus it is almost a necessity that, when illusions about the role of money turn out to be in vain, planning returns to its former methods. Even if it does not use so many indices as before, or even if it presents the planning stipulations as guidelines rather than as compulsory ones, it nevertheless seeks once more to regulate economic activity in detail, by using material indices. (In the 1960s, when the prevailing system was essentially one of self-accounting, the expression of production targets in material terms turned up again and again, and the methods of allocation in material units by and large survived.)

We may conclude, then, that only the realisation of the principles of the new economic reform can really relieve planning of its detail work and enable it to deal with genuine long-term planning and questions of perspective, instead of balancing the books to create equilibrium. This becomes an actual possibility if the autarkic, "material balance" approach to planning is replaced by the attempt to achieve dynamic development, and if economic management gives up its autarkic practices in reality, not only in announcements.

(2) The particular relation of the three basic economic systems to *financial management* is perhaps even more important. In the "administrative" management system, the role of financial management is simply to carry out budgeting activities. On the basis of detailed prescriptions, it has to ensure that directives in all spheres of the economy are fulfilled. As with planning, the emphasis is on detailed accounting, on stipulated norms which cover absolutely everything, and on checking that they are fulfilled. However, financial supervision in the strict sense of the term is frequently driven into the background by the emphasis on the role of material indices, and is often in fact directly tied to them.

In the self-accounting system, the management of enterprise finances operating on the *khozraschot* principle becomes distinct from that which deals with the state budgetary institutions. This is the beginning of the advance of specialised finance organs at the expense of the planning apparatuses, which under the "administrative" management system had almost total power. In accordance with the character of the economic system, what comes to the fore is the determination of production prices based on an *ex-ante* and *ex-post* calculation of production costs, on which the entire self-accounting system is built. Profits, the reduction of production costs and increasing productivity are all tied to the specialised management function of pricing. The system cannot be understood without an understanding of the mechanism of pricing itself, together with its actual and implicit consequences. This is why even under the self-accounting system, financial management may appear as a real, direct power from the enterprises' point of view. Generally speaking, producer and service prices are the result of bargaining between different institutions. Financial plans are co-ordinated at *direct* talks, where maximum or close to maximum bonuses and shares of profit are aimed at. In the course of the year, or by means of annual adjustments, actual reality is made to approximate to the concept. But this is still a hidden, disguised form of management; and in addition, it may appear that the old hierarchy has remained unchanged at the various levels of management, with the planning offices at the summit of this hierarchy.

Only the third basic economic system, that which is based on

153

socialist enterprise, can create the opportunities for financial organs to operate with a dual function, and to manage economic life openly and without covering things up. The dual function is (a) to work out what are known as indirect controls, and to work out economic tools which, when applied, make it possible to realise the aims that have been developed during the planning process; and (b) to utilise financial operations (e.g. the granting of credit) which do not automatically follow plans going into every detail, but require special economic decisions from the financial organs. One of the most fundamental effects of the new economic reform is that the planning function is concentrated to a large extent on prospective planning and, within this, on defining aims; in the meantime, it gives to the control apparatus and to specialised financial management the job of working out the tools needed in order to realise the aims, together with the practical performance of the economic transactions which are necessary for production and distribution. In this latter respect, however, a special contradiction develops between socialist enterprise operating under the principles of the new economic system and the banks, since the latter continue to operate under the "administrative" management system. So while a by no means unimportant part of the companies develop into real "enterprises", the banking organisations remain a budgetary institution. This contradiction can hardly be solved without the creation of banking enterprises; these need not break into the government's financial monopoly, just as the foreign trade monopoly does not suffer from extending export-import rights to various kinds of enterprise. In this respect, a distinction can be made between *government* monopoly and *institutional* monopoly.

(3) The effects of the three economic systems can perhaps be most clearly seen in the field of *labour management*, and of the labour and wages subsystem. One of the necessary consequences of the "administrative" management system is the formation of a "tariff system" (i.e. standard wage grades) for labour, combined with fixed numbers of employees, which in fact tries to realise its aims through the stipulation and control of material indices. In practice, this means that the central plans not only stipulate the numbers of employees for enterprises and institutions but they also, in the form of compulsory stipulations, centrally determine the various tariff groups; in the same way, they stipulate the maximum and minimum wages payable to each group, while there are regulations to fix the particular form of wage payment to be applied, and attempts are made to work out the "basic norms" centrally. In Hungary, this system was valid until 1956, i.e. as long

154

as the "administrative" management system played the dominant role in the economy. After this, largely because the principles of self-accounting began to come into force in Hungarian industry, the system of controlling average wage levels was introduced. This fits coherently into the self-accounting system, since it gives the enterprise a relatively large amount of independence where wages are concerned, while simultaneously ensuring (by means of stipulating what the average wages must be) a fixed level of wage costs proportionate to production prices: this comes about through the decision-making processes of specialised management organs, and it is the foundation of self-accounting. It is quite obvious that the stipulation of average wage levels cannot be dispensed with in a system that is still based on self-accounting. This is not a question of "good" versus "bad", as the economic debates have suggested, but simply an unavoidable necessity. Unless the essence of the economic system is changed, there can only be retreats to different, more detailed kinds of regulator (for example, the constant readjustment of stipulations for numbers of employees). This has occurred whenever it has become obvious that the regulating role of money in the economy has not produced satisfactory results precisely because pricing has taken an administrative form.

The new economic reform, in which the principles of socialist enterprise can be realised, provides the only opportunity for economic management to dispense both with stipulating wages from the centre and with more detailed stipulations such as those for numbers of employees. This process is still a very slow-moving one, even today. This indicates that the effects of the economic reform have been confirmed only to a small extent; because of this, and because of the deep attachment to what one is accustomed to (which is a very frequent phenomenon), the realisation of new solutions takes place only slowly. Above all, this is why the implementation of the principles of a labour and wages subsystem under the new system has not yet been achieved. The process is also slowed down by the fact that those in the labour affairs apparatus, which was necessarily oversized under the "administrative" management and self-accounting systems, are afraid of losing their functions.

From what I have described above, it can be concluded that our industry necessarily contains elements of all three economic systems, and that there will continue to be fields, even in the long-term perspective, where one or the other system plays the dominant role; planning, financial and manpower management will also remain equally heterogeneous (as will the subsystems of invesment and technical development, which are not discussed here). The fact is that we can find elements of all three solutions: for example, on the wages issue we can find the tariff or "wage-grades" system alongside both the stipulation of average wage levels and planned regulation of manpower and wages by indirect means. Experiments in *homogenisation* of these elements can be found in virtually all the economic subsystems: but they do not accord with actual necessity, nor with the principles of rationality.

The development of economic consciousness and the basic types of economic system

The interest relations of the forms of economic management which have developed in the various institutions and enterprises very substantially, according to which of the three economic systems is involved. This is of course expressed in the ideologies they represent, and which permeate economic thinking or (in other words) economic consciousness. It would perhaps be best to begin with the realm of appearances, which is something that everyone has experienced and is therefore easily proven, and then to approach the area which is more difficult to reach or to accept, i.e. the interest relations and particularity of management.

In order to simplify this realm of appearances, which even by its mere existence is so complex, I have tried to find the most important guiding principles which are motivated by the ideology of all three economic systems. If we compress the characteristic features of the individual economic systems into a single description for each, then we can say that the "administrative" management system is characterised by the *quantitative approach*, the self-accounting system by the attempt to *reduce production costs and improve the quality of commodities*, and the socialist enterprise system by the attempt to increase the *efficiency* of enterprises and of the national economy. The mixture of economic thinking with ideology (which has always emphasised its own scientific and rational foundations) is not only a consistent part and product of the individual economic systems, but is closely connected with the socio-economic positions of the individual socialist countries.

The postwar reconstruction period, the failure to exploit opportunities because of the extensive development of industry, the underdevelopment of the management system—all these things were factors which acted in favour of the "administrative" management system and the role of the quantitative approach. I am not saying that there were no other alternatives, only that under these circumstances this solution undoubtedly had the best chance. The "quantitative approach" and its qualitative supplement, the principle of "planned and balanced development", gave rise to mystifying attempts to ensure an autarkic material balance at all costs and, as a direct result of all this, the attempt to achieve autarky in general.

The emergence of the self-accounting system, whether in theory or in practice, is connected with changes in socio-economic circumstances, with the arrival of a situation where labour has to be economised, and with the emergence of special apparatuses capable of carrying out a higher level of management tasks. In these circumstances, the problem of reducing production costs comes almost automatically to the forefront, as well as the designation of indices which express efficiency (e.g. enterprise profits, production value per worker or per man-hour—though it has been proved in economic terms that neither one nor the other expresses the actual social efficiency of labour). Experience has proved that all of these indices can be substantially improved by lowering the quality of the products; and if the market does not have the power to prevent it, this phenomenon will increase, whatever bureaucratic controls are introduced to stop it. This is why the demand to reduce production costs and to improve the quality of the product becomes a combined one: it is an indication of the effort to overcome the contradictions between them.

In comparison to the quantitative approach, this ideology enabled the economic sciences to develop and to blossom out. But the essence of pricing (administrative pricing) remained taboo, and distorted the indices which were intended to indicate productivity, profits and national economic efficiency, by turning them into fictitious figures. At the same time, this often turned economic and mathematical methods which had won international fame into senseless abstractions. The practical critique proved to be stronger than the theoretical critique (though the latter too was expressed with increasing confidence, with the work of Tibor Laska first being responsible in Hungary); it increasingly demanded that a distinction be made between, on the one hand, the enterprise profits and the growth in productivity, etc., which occur with "administrative" producer and service prices, and, on the other hand, the actual enterprise efficiency that occurs with (economic) market prices.

The development of the practical critique was assisted by the general recognition of the fact that the economy was not sufficiently effective in relation to the dynamics of development. This process of realistic self-analysis was furthered by the fact that a comparatively large proportion of our products are exported, and thus that the actual social usefulness and enterprise activity is, in the strict sense of the term, *revalued* for various foreign trade transactions, and particularly for ones with the West. It became more tangible from day to day just how unequal were the quantities of labour we were exchanging, at our own expense. In this respect one of the biggest difficulties was caused by the fact that the role of export enterprises in the institutional structure made the confrontation a very indirect one, and therefore it took a long time for the effects to be felt.

The ideological and practical realisation of the "socialist enterprise" system, in which efficiency is no longer measured by administrative (bureaucratic) prices but by market (economic) ones, gave a new direction to the development of economic thinking. It gave rise to the figure of the "enlightened economist", who either directly or indirectly demands a radical revision of economic thinking and of the ideology which largely determines it. This kind of economist even attacks certain theses which had previously been considered absolutely unshakeable, such as the guarantee of full employment, or preferential pricing for basic consumer goods. If we look only at this aspect of it, this may perhaps seem to constitute a danger to the elaboration and realisation of socialist alternatives of social progress. Nevertheless, the appearance of this trend in economics promises a comparatively rapid escape for socialism from the depressing law of economic necessity. It projects conditions under which the increased dynamics of development will create the material foundation for the further realisation of socialist principles.

However, we must also take note of the fact that the economies of the European socialist countries cannot be homogeneous, but must necessarily retain the elements of all three economic systems. Their emergence and the essentially different roles which they play depend on the different national economic and industrial branches and the peculiarites of these branches. This means that all three methods of approach will necessarily be retained and reproduced in economic thinking, but none will be able to become totally dominant. We can assume that in the future, progress will not appear in the form of one direction being substituted for another, but that they will develop in confrontation with each other, without the possibility of a monopoly appearing. And in the final analysis, in spite of the contradictions with each other, which will

lead to sharp and frequently serious conflict, they will serve to
reinforce the realisation of socialist values and the rational point
of view.

X: Bureaucratism and the Social Pathology of the Administration

"The bureaucracy is a circle from which no one can escape. Its hierarchy is a hierarchy of knowledge. The top entrusts the understanding of detail to the lower levels, whilst the lower levels credit the top with understanding of the general, and so all are mutually deceived."

Marx, *Contribution to the Critique of Hegel's "Philosophy of Law"*

Bureaucratism as a structural problem

As I have tried to illustrate in several studies, both in societies which preserve private property and in those which have already abolished it, special apparatuses within the administration and management of society nowadays play an ever greater role, and their influence extends into ever wider areas of social life. It seems that, in the developing societies, the execution of management functions requires to an increasing extent that those who undertake them should have the necessary specialised knowledge, that they should carry out their tasks both as a vocation and as their principal occupation. That is, the fulfilment of their functions should be part and parcel of their very existence in the given structure of society.

When observing the exceptionally complex and contradictory changes in the course of which management by the laity comes to be replaced by professional management, everyday thinking often only grasps those surface phenomena which have a negative implication for mankind. It is in this way that the pejorative stereotype of management develops. It finds expression, among other things, in the negative ring of the word "bureaucracy", despite the fact that sociology generally uses the concept without any value judgement, and identifies it directly with the concept of administration. For my own part I do not accept this identification. Keeping myself to Marx's intepretation, I link the concept of bureaucracy to that specific *essential* relationship which ties the apparatuses of management to society or to its different classes, and whose specific essence lies in the particular interests of the administration.

Whatever opinions they express about the apparatuses of administration and management, and however much they might be convinced of their necessity and efficiency, the professors of social science cannot deny the existence of these negative characteristics. These characteristics, the existence of which public opinion also clearly senses, can be best understood under the general term of bureaucratism. In answer to this generally experienced phenomenon, there are essentially three standpoints which social scientists can adopt: (a) to consider them as individual or personal mistakes which can be overcome by education, or perhaps by some kind of deterrence, since they are not essential attributes of the administration; (b) to see them as characteristic features of an administration that is not yet fully developed, features which are not characteristic of the ideal type of administration (bureaucracy), but negative aspects which can be eliminated as administration is modernised; or, to follow an argument that is not essentially different from the former, they can be seen as the results of a disproportionately swollen bureaucracy, results which will disappear if the disproportions themselves can be ended; (c) finally, to see in these negative factors a structural phenomenon whose existence is due to the nature of the administration, that is, primarily to the essential relation which binds it to society, or rather to its various classes and strata.

The first of these conceptions has always reflected an apologetic intention, and it still does today. Whether this conception should be regarded as progressive or reactionary depends on whether the administrative apparatuses that it seeks to defend themselves serve the cause of social progress, or whether they allow the old and now superseded state of affairs to be maintained at all costs, and the different types of bureaucratic power to be preserved, even when their supersession has become historically possible. This is similar to the way that the administration of the Prussian state, which was defended in an indirect way by a large group of young Hegelians, came in fact, with its own particular interest, to oppose almost every progressive endeavour. It was for precisely this reason that the desire of Ruge and his associates to serve the progress of society turned, before long, into its very opposite. It was in fact in opposition to Ruge that Marx could write the following: "The *contradiction* between the purpose and goodwill of the administration, on the one hand, and its means and possibilities, on the other hand, cannot be abolished by the state without the latter abolishing itself, for it is *based* on this contradiction."[56]

161

Attitudes similar to those of the Young Hegelians have often cropped up in the course of history, both before and since then. This is primarily because, when we recognise a régime to be progressive in terms of our own system of values, we are frequently inclined to consider it, and the entire institutional network it comprises, as the only true solution. We then come to seek the source of its faults not within it, but within men.

The second approach—concentrating on the specific features of the institutional system of bureaucratism—is characteristic of the empirical trend which dominates bourgeois sociology today, especially in the USA. That is to say, if it is in the first place organisational mistakes and shortcomings, and not essential structural causes, that bring about the negative characteristics, then recommendations based on appropriate analyses would appear to be very promising—and these cannot do without the sociological approach. Thus, alongside other branches of the social sciences, sociology can also have a place in raising the efficiency of management.

Since the turn of the century, bureaucratism as a negative feature of the administration has been a much analysed theme in American sociology, even on a theoretical level. This is perhaps because, in the USA, the development of bureaucracy cannot look back to so long a historical past as in Europe or Asia, and only a short period of time separates the almost completely bureaucratised world of the thirties from the democratic attitude of New England.

In bourgeois social science, according to Merton, the revelation of the pathological consequences of bureaucracy is associated with the development of such concepts as Veblen's "trained incapacity", Dewey's "occupational psychosis", and Warnotte's "professional deformation". In actual fact all these concepts are related to the one-sidedness which is demanded by routine work but has at the same time become overdeveloped, and which thus shows itself incapable of rational behaviour in a changing situation. The essence of bureaucracy is thus shown to be a negative trait which appears in the individual, but has its roots within the organisation. Merton[57] has developed this view further. He does not consider the negative characteristics of administration to be simply the harmful effect on the individual of either an "underorganised" or an "overorganised" bureaucracy. Instead, he emphasises the nature of the organisation itself, in which the various interests of the administration also have a role to play.

In my approach, while I can in many respects make use of the concrete studies of bourgeois sociology, and Merton's approach

162

too, in analysing the social pathology of bureaucracy, I am never-theless opposed to them. I do not identify bureaucratism either with the negative effects of the organisation on individuals, or with the nature of the organisation itself (its dysfunction). I consider it to be a phenomenon which is *rooted in the essential social relations* and which can only be destroyed by a change in these relations. It is only in this approach that I can see a way to discovering, on the basis of the marxist social viewpoint, the causes of these phenomena.

This does not of course mean that it would not be possible to struggle against bureaucratism, even within the existing socio-economic system, and with a greater or lesser degree of success, using any one of these approaches. We must recognise the limits of our activity, especially in relation to socialism. Above all else we must be aware that the fight against bureaucratism has to be carried on with unceasing drive: victory over it, over its existence, is inconceivable until socialism reaches a higher stage, that is, to put it more concretely, until the essential administration of society is no longer carried out by special apparatuses.

It follows from the above considerations that when I examine the social pathology of the administrative apparatuses I shall exclude those negative consequences which are not directly related to the mode of existence of these institutions (consequences which are better classified as subjective or chance phenomena). This is not to deny that, in their concrete appearance, structural "mis-takes" will in fact always take on the stamp of the personalities of the people working within the administration. Indeed, this can sometimes create an extreme distortion of certain phenomena, while at other times significantly alleviating them. For me as a sociologist, however, it is not the individual appearance of the "mistakes" that is important. The important thing for me is the common element which is present both in the grotesquely deformed bureaucratic phenomena and in those which take on a milder form.

The price of order—specific conservatism

A desire to maintain the existing state of affairs, to a greater or lesser degree, invariably arises within the administrative appara-tuses and management—once, that is, they have developed beyond the *in statu nascendi* condition, and have reached an initial stage in their development. This arises from the inner necessity created by some particular interest, such as the frequently experienced thirst for expansion. It is for precisely this reason that administration is not simply "the party of order" but, far more than that, "the organisation of order".

The scientific and theoretical root of this is the belief in the ideal of a harmonious and contradiction-free society or institution. This idea was formulated by Thorstein Veblen, who was the founder of the sociology of institutions, and for whom the central category was adaptation or adjustment. The abolition of conflicts, or rather their filing away into the category of "Bad", is most commonly found in the thinking of the managers of large economic organisations. They conceive of the organisation as a disciplined and integrated system, every member of which identifies, or rather should identify, completely with the aims of the organisation.

This attitude, which recognises the right of existence of only one type of answer to every question, is especially characteristic of the state administrations that have been established in bourgeois society. In the history of bureaucracy, it is here that practical conservatism first joins forces with ideological dogmatism.

"The bureaucratic spirit", writes Marx, "is a jesuitical, theological spirit through and through. The bureaucrats are the jesuits and theologians of the state. The bureaucracy is *la république prêtre.*"[58]

Modern bourgeois sociology senses the damaging side of this striving towards monolithic thought and behaviour. While Merton, in his study of the relationship between social structure and *anomie*, gives a typology of the mode of individual adaptation to the organisation and thus follows the Veblen tradition in many respects, he stresses at the same time that although the innovating spirit is effective in society on the basis of cultural values, it inevitably meets with resistance from institutionalisation. For bureaucratic thought—which, I stress again, need not necessarily reign within the organisation—every new idea or solution constitutes a threat. In the majority of cases, the internal allocation of responsibilities, and the maintenance of the status system, are more important than any organisational aims.

In dynamic societies, however, whatever structural factors there may be to support it, this conservatism cannot become dominant, for in such societies individual institutions are forced to react to technical innovations with the necessary responsiveness, even at the price of renouncing their own existence. An effort to smash this frequently experienced aspect of bureaucratism, its practical conservatism and ideological dogmatism, or in other words its "theological spirit" in the marxist sense, can be recognised in modern societies; not only in the socialist countries that have abolished private property, but also those that retain it. On this basis, modern capitalist bureaucracy develops its own particular spirit. It is conservative in its view of social and political relations, and in questions of its own organisation, but at the same time it can give effective encouragement to technical progress, at least to the extent that it serves the growth of profit and, along with this, the expansion of the power and spheres of influence of some individual institutions. Under socialism, however, technical progress is encouraged as far as the interests of the institution allow or require it.

Single individuals can break out of this ring of social constraint, can become revolutionaries (there are many such cases) or, with a little imagination, they can look for even more ingenious forms of liberation, like Kafka's clerk who changed into an insect before setting out for the office. However, the managerial bureaucracy as a social group necessarily remains essentially conservative in its relationship to the social and political structure, and even in its view of its own organisational problems. Naturally the ideology of bureaucracy does not recognise either practical conservatism or ideological dogmatism as structural phenomena. At most, both are seen as symptomatic of an inexpert and not yet fully developed management apparatus. What is more, it gives birth to an outlook which declares management and the administration to be the most important representatives of social progress.

The completion of this function falls in no small way upon technocratic theories of various kinds. These serve, at one and the same time, as the ideological justification of the separateness of management and administration. They expect the advance of technocracy and specialised knowledge to overcome all the negative phenomena characteristic of bureaucracy, and they attach particularly high hopes to the ways by which they think conservatism can be completely overcome.

This problem, which has been analysed so much in capitalist societies, is not unknown to those who deal with the sociological problems of the administrative apparatuses that have been established in socialist societies. Here too, illusions form as to the development of an "intelligent", "enlightened" administration, which will soon be able to solve every social problem that faces us today. In reality, however, even the most enlightened administrations are inseparably linked to particular interests. This phenomenon is in no small way responsible for the fact that the replacement of an already developed economic system by a new one becomes an exceptionally complicated social problem, and leads to unavoidable social conflicts. No economic system is ever simply a more or less coherent manifestation of certain managerial methods and a system of vertically and horizontally linked institutions. It is rather, primarily, a developed power structure, the functioning of which is in fact simply the exercise of power that has been divided up in a particular way between its institutions and departments.

Thus every idea of reform inevitably finds itself in opposition not simply to established habits but also to the power structure in which innovation promises to bring about significant changes. This naturally bears within itself not only the possibility of stubborn opposition, but also the source of victory for the new, at least if those who are likely to gain the most from the victory of the new consciously take up the challenge and, allying themselves with those who see the new as representing a general interest, are able to overcome the opposition which rises against it. The basis of the opposition is, incidentally, more often a sort of vague existential fear—which almost always appears in an ideological garb—than any conscious foresight of the negative effects which the changes will have on the particular interests of individual groups.

The interrelation between conservatism and progress in the administrative apparatuses of socialist societies becomes even more complicated (if that is possible) in specific but decisive questions such as that of technical development. The connections between the power structure and the different kinds of technical changes are much more indirect and difficult to recognise than in the case of reforms carried out in the economic system, and it is much more difficult to find ideological arguments against them.

Technical development and technical and technological innovations in general do not meet with such open opposition within management as do organisational changes. At the same time, however, in most cases no notable material interest is associated with them, and therefore significant social forces cannot be aligned with them either. Practical experience shows that if we disregard the motivations dictated by recognised social interests, that which primarily helps technical development is generally the commitment of experts to their profession.

If the dynamism of technical development is not tied up with any other particular institutional or individual material interest (as we must suppose to be the case in economic systems based on either "state administrative" or "self-accounting" principles) then, in fields managed by the specialised apparatuses, its fate is decided primarily by the place which experts who identify with the development of their profession are allotted in the power structure, and by the support they get from those whose occupations do not tie them to narrow particular interests (that is, by the forces "above" and "outside" the management apparatuses).

But we must not make an absolute value even out of the trivial sounding truth of "progress fired by professional dedication". Professional dedication often conceals an over-evaluation of a person's own ability, and under such circumstances it often happens that even the very best experts oppose the employment of the most developed machines and methods, and force those they have themselves produced on to the national economy. In his recent book, Domokos Varga describes a shocking case of men who were dedicated to their profession in this way, and who for many years hindered the purchase of safety equipment required for new machines on the forestry estates, because they were confident that they could make their own invention to solve the problem. In this case the "waiting" was accompanied not only by material costs, but also by damage to the health of a great many people.

"Homo Hierarchicus"

"The office universe which, among other things, Kafka has described, this universe of formalities, of absurd gestures, of purposeless behaviour, is essentially masculine. . . . Man's enterprises are at once projects and evasions: he lets himself be smothered by his career and his 'front'; he often becomes self-important, serious."

Simone de Beauvoir, *The Second Sex*

As we have already seen above, the source of bureaucratism is generally nothing but a feature of the administrative apparatuses which is either necessary for their successful operation, or is grossly exaggerated, or is developed to proportions in which it is not only unnecessary but has a directly harmful effect. In this way, something born of rationalism produces irrationalism. Something originally designed to serve efficiency becomes the source of quite fruitless activities. Such an oddity can be well illustrated with the problem of hierarchy and hierarchisation which, at least in the dimension of power relations, of sub- and super-ordination, is inseparably linked with the development and existence of the

167

administration.

This is not a typical characteristic of the initial period of development of the administration, of its *in statu nascendi* condition, either in capitalist or in socialist relations. This former condition, out of which the hierarchy of administration grows, if it is not one of equality is at least a different type of inequality from the one the new system brings with it. Here in Hungary, for example, capitalist society recruited its civil servants from the nobility, and at the beginning this common origin created a certain equality in the face of the minority from bourgeois backgrounds, and again and again broke through the dividing walls of the hierarchy. This "as yet unhierarchised state" is even more perceptible in the development of the administration in socialist societies, where the most important roles were played by people accustomed to the egalitarianism of the labour movement, and particularly by workers who understandably found it hard to accept the necessity for hierarchisation.

Immediately after the assumption of power in Hungary, in the years 1945-50, the party organisations represented very important tendencies against hierarchisation. Within the party organisations, particularly in this period, party members were not only equals according to organisational rules, but besides this their social prestige was in no way determined by their place in the hierarchy of the administration. More important for them was the respect that they won within either the party or the movement, and this was something they were usually able to assert within the administration too. The process of hierarchisation, which came unavoidably later, naturally cannot be considered as a fortuitous or simply negative phenomenon. This process was made obviously necessary by the drive for efficiency of the administration, and by setting the strengthening of discipline as an aim. The latter seemed simply inconceivable (at least at that stage of development) without the establishment of relations of sub- and superordination.

The question is not one of the necessity of setting up hierarchies as such, but rather, partly one of whether hierarchisation in particular organisations surpasses the optimal level of efficiency (that is, whether excessive hierarchisation has occurred), and partly one of the nature of its negative effects on people, and on the relations between them, of the level of hierarchy still considered necessary. If we consider the wider sphere of social relations (specialised knowledge, income, cultural level) which play a role in the life of the institutions, and not just the relations of sub- and super-ordination, then modern organisations look not so much like pyramids, as like nets with several bunches. We must take this into account when we discuss the question of the necessity of hierarchies. If in several respects (in different dimensions) some sort of hierarchisation does actually come about, then it cannot usually be arranged simply in one dimension, that is, according to the hierarchy of relations of sub- and super-ordination.

Of course, it is also conceivable that we could rank every important difference within a single dimension, on the basis of some artificially contrived value system. But this would in no way bring us any nearer to the real situation than the empirical schools of bourgeois sociology which construct a one-dimensional hierarchical social structure, which results in just as many strata as they like, from "upper-upper" to "lower-lower". This, however, is a creation of the consciousness of *homo hierarchicus*. It is by no means simply a kind of passive reflection of the outside world; it is a stimulus to all sorts of activity which seeks to mould the world to a consciousness created by particular interest. All this will be seen differently by someone who is neither an external spectator nor an active creator of this one-dimensionality, but who, working in a particular apparatus of the administration, is a subject that suffers under these tendencies. For him, if he has not yet become a man of the hierarchy, a *homo hierarchicus*, this one-dimensionality is a prison, especially if he senses the necessity multi-dimensionality of his nature and of his social relations, and if, in his system of values, the preservation and development of this becomes the highest aim by which he hopes to realise his fully human nature.

The recognition of the multi-dimensional nature of society and its institutions, however, is not just a precondition for the development of the individual in the marxist sense, and for the development of a more adequate picture of society better corresponding to reality. It is also a precondition for making the individual institutions and organisations more efficient. General experience shows that the more developed an organisation, the more likely it is to be characterised by one-dimensional hierarchisation which, in the course of its development, it strives to throw off like a piece of clothing it has grown out of. Practical experience contradicts at every step the usefulness of one-dimensional hierarchisation, and bears witness to the necessity for a multi-dimensional conception. R. L. Simpson, for example, shows that in the factory he studied, horizontal relationships were more clearly defined than vertical ones.[59] At the same time, however, we can often hear the opinion that within the organisation it is almost exclusively vertical relations which play any significant role, and that it is in the relationship of sub- and super-ordination that the significant portion of communication and information-flow within the organisation takes place. This view likewise influences the ruling tendencies of both organisational theory and legal theory, and not least the practice of management.

An outlook that would turn everything into a hierarchy requires a system of establishing prestige within individual institutions which is unambiguously linked to the position occupied within the hierarchy. Thus it completely ignores the fact that a large part is played in the established order of prestige by the personal prestige of individual men, which is made up of many components, and which often upsets the hierarchical order. The man of the hierarchy, however, does not bother about this. His sole desire is to rise higher, and he believes that by so doing he will increase his social esteem as well. He almost instinctively rejects any information which might undermine these convictions or his ability to maintain them. This outlook even seems to get support from some trends in sociology. Following a Weberian typology, the prestige order of organisations is compared to those of traditional and charismatic systems, but still linked clearly to the hierarchy of formal organisations. People who work within the administration and management are seen as building up the prestige of their boss or bosses in a similar way as vassals increased that of their masters, or disciples that of the charismatic prophets. However, this conception cannot even be realised in rudimentary organisations since, because of the complexity of social relations, personal prestige cannot be aligned exactly with the hierarchical order. Moreover, in more modern organisations too, structural causes have prevented the striving for hierarchisation from being justifiable, and this is precisely because of the development of the horizontal relations mentioned above.

For *homo hierarchicus*, however, not only is prestige aligned with the hierarchical order, but so too is knowledge. The higher one stands in the hierarchy, the more one knows, or at least ought to know. In reality, however, especially in modern organisations, we do not find that knowledge is directly linked to position in the hierarchy. Usually the person who occupies a higher position does not have to have simply more knowledge, but rather different knowledge. For example, in every field of their operations, efficient administrators have to be able to call on the services of subordinates who have more specialised knowledge than they. In modern administrative organisations, it is not only specialised knowledge that cannot be placed in a hierarchy within the dimension of relations of sub- and super-ordination, but also intellectual ability, "intelligence". Moreover, this sort of hierarchisation cannot be experienced either at the level of Being [*Sein*] or in the dimension of Ought [*Sollen*]. This is especially easy to see if we accept the growing role of experts and researchers in administration as a necessity, for the varied tasks of co-ordination and supervision are carried out "above" them, by people whose intellectual level, for sheer practical reasons, is no more developed than theirs.

Thus a new contradiction arises within bureaucratic organisations. If hierarchisation goes beyond the requisite limits and justifiable dimensions, the expert who enters the administration is sooner or later forced to give up the work he has been trained for, and with which he may largely identify himself, and to take on responsibility for a set of tasks which he is not properly trained to perform. The principles of administration and, amongst them, the concept of *homo hierarchicus* are gaining ground with great speed even within scientific research. Here too it is usual to try to relate not only specialised knowledge, but also research ability as well, to the hierarchical order established within the dimension of the relations of domination. This is shown for example by the phenomenon, which can be experienced in many places, of relating the attainment of scientific rank to the position occupied in the hierarchy of the research administration.

Thus one of the most important and harmful consequences of over-hierarchisation, particularly from the point of view of the efficiency of the organisation, develops: the exclusion of the expert from the organisation. This can be understood in two ways: (a) if he really is a dedicated expert, then he will leave because he is unable to bear the one-sided hierarchical order of the organisation, and he will seek a place of work where he can free himself, to some degree, from being ordered into a rigid hierarchy. Alternatively, if his expert knowledge is after all necessary in certain dimensions, then it will ensure him a higher prestige and income than his position in the hierarchy of relations of sub- and super-ordination would justify. (In practice it is as often as not the latter that happens.) (b) The second way of losing the qualities of experts occurs when the expert accommodates himself to the hierarchy, and when, over a period of time, his professional qualities (dedication, motivations, aspirations) become a thing of the past. Indeed, it is often considered a good thing if a knowledge and flair for administration and management develop in their place.

171

Social problems of a similar scale arise if the answer to the question "who is right?" is slotted into the hierarchical order. Great emphasis is very often laid upon this managerial principle in the higher levels of management of institutions. It is a principle which not only wounds human dignity, but which also causes serious difficulties even when looked at strictly from the point of view of the efficiency of the organisation. Before all else, it is this that gives birth to conformism. In such institutions the subordinates become convinced, on the basis of their everyday experience, that they can never be right against their bosses. Because of this, they give up any striving for the truth, or at least any attempt to tell it, and they accommodate themselves uncritically to the value system of their bosses, trying to think with their bosses' heads and feel with their bosses' hearts. This situation can often seem favourable to the managers, and its main danger lies precisely in this. It is due to this that the right to recognise the truth becomes tied to the position occupied in the hierarchy just like, let us say, the right to the use of a car. This too can appear as the most important and indispensable precondition of order in organisations. In fact, however, it is no more than a means of establishing conformism and conservatism, which inevitably reduces efficiency.

One of the typical characteristics of the ideology of over-hierarchisation is that it prefers to base wage differentials not on specialised knowledge or the nature of the work performed, but on the position occupied in the organisation taken as a whole, that is, on the different levels of the hierarchy. In the eyes of *homo hierarchicus* the greatest injustice is committed if, for some reason or other, the distribution of incomes does not follow the order of rank in the organisation and the general tendency to associate this with the distribution of responsibility. (It is a common experience of sociological enquiry, to find that people working at the highest level of the administration consider the degree of responsibility to be the most important criterion in the establishment of wage differentials.) The organisational interest, however, often directly requires that individual incomes should diverge from the hierarchy, especially in institutions where the introduction of researchers and experts with outstanding knowledge is necessary. Naturally this does not mean that there might not be some areas of our national economy where it would be a good idea to raise the vertical wage differentials. This would primarily be the case in areas where the occupation of higher posts really does entail serious responsibility. However, we should not assume for a moment that at *every* similar level the *real* responsibilities and risks will be necessarily identical.

172

At the level of directors, for example, it depends (among other things) on the type of economic system that the institution in question is a part of.

One of the most striking signs of over-hierarchisation is the attitude of callous condescension towards the client. This is in fact simply the projection, on to society outside, of an outlook that has developed within the administration, and which reflects the bureaucratic system of dependence. According to this view, the client is an outsider, an alien or lesser being, indeed sometimes simply an ill-intentioned individual to whom the administration, as the possessor of a power bestowed upon it by the whole of society, will stand hierarchically superior whatever happens. In the minds of some civil servants the mystified social interest is as often as not a greater force than any God-ordained monarch or capitalist corporation; nowadays, in socialist society, it has become associated with the prestige, part real and part imagined, that is afforded by position in the hierarchy. And, to make the situation even more grotesque and contradictory, this absolutisation and hierarchisation of the relations of domination is often more strongly adhered to by those at the lower levels of the hierarchy than by those at higher levels. The former want, as it were, to get their own back on the clients because, within the administrative system itself, they have no real possibilities for decision-making. Thus we are presented with the sergeant who is brutal towards his men, or the porter who is rude to the clients.

A special case of this relationship arises when the client *in his capacity as client* is not simply an ordinary citizen, but someone who occupies a specific position in the hierarchical order of another organisation. Such a person has claims to a "partner" relationship precisely because the other institution cannot use just any pretext to ignore his own prestige. An extremely complex mechanism is at work here, one which will completely ignore some of these claims while admitting others. Nor is it so rare for cases to arise when "over-evaluation" occurs, and the client comes to feel that he is no longer just a partner, "one amongst equals", but a person endowed with some special power, whose every wish becomes a command in the other organisation. This is, of course, harmful to the hierarchy of the bureaucracy compressed into a single institution, but in point of fact it accepts it nevertheless, as a kind of external constraint which must be complied with, and through which the inner hierarchy is complemented by external factors. Possibly there will be the occasional clerk who, identifying himself with his own institution, may rebel a little against this. In the end,

173

however, he will sooner or later come to regard it as part and parcel of the "natural order", just like the order of his own institution.

Thus even in the offices and workplaces, people usually find themselves in a multi-dimensional world, in which (a) they occupy a particular position in the hierarchy of workplace organisations, (b) they are partners and sometimes even persons of rank in relation to the orders of other organisations, and (c) they are simple clients, sometimes just because a particular institution does not recognise the prestige they have gained elsewhere. Hierarchy does not just develop in the realm of the workplace, however, but also in many other institutions and organisations in society (in the party, in social organisations, etc.), and often even in groups based on affection and friendship.

This is one of the very things which itself offers resistance to the one-dimensionality of bureaucracy. It can hardly be doubted that, at least in the final analysis, it will enable the struggle for the recognition of the multi-dimensionality of society to be victorious. *Homo hierarchicus,* the man who thinks in one dimension, who is the prototype of today's organisation man, will be made redundant once and for all.

And perhaps it is not entirely utopian, either, to believe that multi-dimensionality will finally diminish the role of hierarchisation itself, and thereby create a situation where man, having matured into an individual personality, can no longer be made to fit into hierarchies.

The "Organisation Man"

This concept was introduced by Whyte, who meant by it that bureaucratically organised administration and management create, or have already created, their own type of man. Considering the level to which man has risen, and the possibilities he has won for developing his personality, this type is a clearly pathological phenomenon, and would be so even if its operation could be shown to be in no way dysfunctional or ineffective. Whyte's "organisation men" are in fact those who "have left home, spiritually as well as physically, to take the vows of organisation life, and it is they who are the mind and soul of our great self-perpetuating institutions."[60]

In this approach the "organisation man", while being recognised as an element supporting the institution, is nevertheless a negative type because, like the sick horse in veterinary books, he carries within himself all the typical diseases which can affect the personality in an organisation. This also means that the real "flesh and blood" person who works in management is never an "organisation man" in fact: but he could become one. In the following, the "qualities" of the organisation man as thus conceived will be seen rather as dangers, and will in no way be taken to indicate an already established condition. But at the same time, it does a man no harm to know about lung disease, cancer or stomach ulcers, even though he does not suffer from any of them—especially if he is threatened by one or another of these diseases because, for some reason or other, he is particularly susceptible to it.

Let us look at some of the symptoms of this many-sided illness:

(1) One of the most serious negative consequences of a bureau-cratised society is the over-exaggeration of the conformity that is necessary both in social life and in activity within the organisation, the development of "conformism". Marx himself brilliantly analysed this characteristic of the bureaucrat: even at the price of completely stifling his own individuality, he will adapt himself to his social environment, and particularly to the real or supposed standards of his bosses, which he accepts uncritically. Under modern capitalism, this trait steps out from the relatively narrow sphere of state administration and becomes conformism in the true sense of the word, a social phenomenon that is valid generally.

Merton sees the structural causes of this phenomenon (which, incidentally, he calls "overconformity") in the following: (a) effective bureaucracy requires reliability of response and unbroken loyalty to the rules; (b) loyalty to the rules leads to them becoming an absolute value: tasks are conceived of not relatively, in relation to the aims, but independently of them; (c) at the same time, those who introduce the general rules cannot conceive of the need for them to be adapted to meet special situations; (d) for this reason, many elements that are effective in general become ineffective in special circumstances.

Conformism, i.e. the over-exaggeration of conformity in this sense, can in no way be considered to have come to an end under socialism. One of the most serious consequences of this phenomenon is "negative selection". by which it is not those who are most suited to the demands of leading fields of work who get into the higher positions, but rather those who have above-average talents in one sole sphere: that of conforming. In such organisations the number of people in leading posts who "know how to behave"

175

is rising, but in close correlation with this, the efficiency of management inevitably declines.

(2) The bureaucratic organisation frequently alienates man from his work. The attainment of success becomes separated from the actual results of work, and appears to be directly identified with rising in the hierarchy. At the same time, there is a view which appears in the value system saying that the really worthy man, the man who is right, is the one who has attained success in this sense.

Within the bureaucratic organisation, the "successful man" is accorded much greater social prestige than the "gifted man" or the man who "knows his job well". If the latter do not get on in the hierarchy, they are often branded with directly pejorative labels, and many people think that they see some pathological symptom in them. It is this condition that Agnes Heller is describing when she writes as follows: "If security is the main aim of life, if men do not take up the struggle, and with it the possibility of failure, then success becomes the only measure of morality. Success becomes synonymous with the good, failure with the bad."[61]

From this point of view, the conception of Robert Presthus is interesting and thought-provoking. He sees three types of identification with large organisations, and he characterises them in the following way: (a) the *riser*, who is able to reconcile his individual aspirations harmoniously with the aims of the organisation; (b) the *indifferent* person, who is equally alienated both from the organisation and from his work, the general type of official to be found in large organisations; (c) the *ambivalent*, whose individual and often very varied expectations are continually colliding against the wall of bureaucracy. For Presthus it is the third type that is pathological. Practical experience shows, however, that the danger to society is hardly any less when the first or the second type becomes a dominant force.

Dahrendorf, for example, asks: "Why are there more suicides in the ranks of those ascending the social hierarchy?"—and the very raising of the question reveals some doubt as to the ability of Presthus's first type of man to free himself of problems. And is the second, the indifferent type, really free of problems either? We can only give a reassuring answer to this question if we consider alienation from his work to be man's normal condition.

(3) Perhaps the greatest danger to the organisation man is that of *depersonalisation*, which affects him in the realm that is so important for him: the realm of work. In the developed bureau-

176

cratic structure, which Galbraith calls the technostructure, there is no longer any form of management with "one-man responsibility". Decisions are no longer individual. All the different questions are decided on within the organisation itself during the preparatory stage, and thus responsibility cannot be individual. We can obviously see the flight to the moon in this way, as the result of a complicated technostructure understood in this sense.

But this phenomenon has also taken on a dominant role in more traditional and heavily concentrated organisations as well. Anthony Sampson, for example, writes that Shell, Unilever or Imperial Tobacco and the other similar multinational economic organisms are mystical phenomena, at whose summit stands a management which is, in the strict sense of the word, anonymous. This change means in fact that power, which in the case of enterprises run by owner-managers was in the hands of individual men, is now held by organisations rather than by individuals. The individual can only exercise his power through an *organisation*, and although it may be under his rule, it also turns him into a creation of its own making.

And for man in this organised world, even if he is at its summit, it is increasingly rare for him to find himself in a situation where he can have decision-making responsibility or even participate in it. In effect, and especially at lower levels, his participation is often limited to activities which on most occasions go no further than the interpretation and application of very detailed regulations. The restriction of autonomy is very often found together with a minimal individual responsibility, and thus Whyte is justified in calling this condition a "system of organised irresponsibility". Because of this, but also because of the influence of hierarchisation, personal relations within the management apparatus almost inevitably become deformed, and this is perhaps one of the most general and most characteristic factors which undermine the human personality in the apparatus. In other words, it is symptomatic of the dysfunction that operates within management itself.

It is almost a commonplace that nowadays man's work relations are of increasing significance in the development of his personality. The actual tasks and conditions of work, and not least the social functions that are actually fulfilled in the workplace, make a deep impression on people's personalities. Those who work within the administrative apparatuses are no exception. But within them, the ability to work in really humanising communities is a much more difficult task, apparently almost an insoluble one.

In administrative apparatuses which are not yet developed,

177

which are *in statu nascendi*, people can still (relatively) "freely love and hate". This was very easily discernible in Hungary: one need only compare the first period of development of the socialist administration, its "heroic age", with the later stages. Expressing ourselves in the language of sociology, this means that in the first period the so-called informal organisation, the system of likes and dislikes, played an exceptionally large part in the organisations. One negative consequence of this state of affairs was the formation of cliques between whom fierce battles broke out, battles which were not only dictated by interests but by heated passions as well. However, this was not the only reason why personal relations were an obstacle to efficiency. Their very existence was like a barricade piled up in defence of the consolidation of hierarchy, and they created difficulties for the change-over from legal formality to actual social reality. As we have already seen, the consolidation of hierarchy, at least in the present circumstances, is to a certain extent indispensable to raising the efficiency of management.

Those who work in management and the administration are, in the sense of Weber's ideal type, people who neither love nor hate, but fulfil their obligations. Even if this is an exaggeration, and if such administrative apparatuses are not to be actually found anywhere in the world, there is nevertheless some truth in the assertion: depersonification is logically attributable to the essential nature of the administration, and is a phenomenon that can be experienced everyday in practice.

The Castle

The efficiency of the administrative and management system appears to run very few risks from its own structural disease, which Marx conceived of as the desire to turn its internal affairs into state secrets. It is precisely this phenomenon which is the most obvious barrier to the expansion of social control and to the prevention which this might achieve of the bureaucratic phenomena becoming dominant. The problem is exacerbated by the fact that the more developed an organisation is, the more capable it is of developing this characteristic. The revolutionary workers' movement has always moved and always will move, against the bureaucratic tendencies which develop within itself. In their various forms, these tendencies are the most important breeding grounds of reformism and revisionism.

178

In modern capitalism a formidable mesh of bureaucratic institutions develops over which neither society nor even the owners have any real control. This is the bureaucratised, depersonalised world which is brought to life in Kafka's *The Castle*. K, the surveyor, wants to get into the castle at all costs so that he can clear up the conditions of his contract, but his every attempt proves fruitless. The lords of the castle remain unknown powers; in the castle, organisation and precision appear to change into their very opposites. The most authoritative of the people he somehow manages to speak with, the Superintendent of the village who is more of a "farmer" than an "official", presents him with the following information about the situation in the castle: "In such a large governmental office as the Count's, it may occasionally happen that one department ordains this, another that; neither knows of the other, and though the supreme control is absolutely efficient, it comes by its nature too late, and so every now and then a trifling miscalculation arises." In this novel it is not simply étatist or managerial bureaucracy that is brought to life, but rather bureaucratised society. It is done with bewildering power. In this world, K, the surveyor, necessarily becomes the plaything of alien forces.

This danger threatens most those administrative apparatuses which display a relatively high level of organisational development, and where the relations of sub- and super-ordination are much more complicated and confusing than they are in simple or even multiple linear systems. In the former case the actual relations are themselves extremely complex, even without attempts to obscure them, and they can only be fathomed out with great difficulty. Thus the working of an organisation can easily seem like "the castle", even if the leaders of the institution do not try to make state secrets out of every internal problem. Such a development becomes almost unavoidable unless the growth of conscious activity is sufficient to make internal problems, and primarily the decision-making processes that go on within the organisation, perceptible and intelligible to the "outside world", to the "lay community". This requires the development of a specific function of the information system, one that has often been neglected in practice: the *general* dissemination of information, both *internally* and *externally*. In contrast to this, organisation theory is often quite content if the workers just get the information sufficient for their own work tasks.

A "corporative" spirit frequently appears within the administration and management, and often finds expression in official declarations. This spirit, openly defending the interests of the organisation, declares internal questions to be secrets that it is not right, or at least not "proper", to talk about in front of out-siders—the uninitiated. This is often as strong a constraint as that which classifies internal problems as state secrets. The punishment for those who break these rules is often no less than that for those who divulge state secrets. In these cases, however, the penalty is usually applied in an indirect fashion. More severe judgement will be passed on some other "crime" or "transgression" the official has committed, and in this way he will be punished for all his disloyalty to the corporative spirit.

This "corporative" spirit is nourished, in a rationalised way, by the clear interest of the organisation. The more that certain ad-ministration and management develop their own special interests, and the more untenable becomes the assertion that they can and must be brought into harmony with the interests of society as a whole, then the greater will be the problem presented by institu-tions developing their own "secrecy systems". This will make it almost impossible to furnish the degree of information about the organisation's activity that is required by reality.

This phenomenon is closely linked to the influence which changes in the economic system can have on the enterprises, especially socialist enterprises operating with a large degree of autonomy. Naturally it would be a mistake to believe that this phenomenon is unknown in the economic systems based on state administration or on self-accounting units. Socialist institutions in these economic systems have also learned very quickly that they should not reveal the extent of their internal reserves to the higher organs of ad-ministration and planning (this has been particularly important in state administrative economic systems). They have also learned, when introducing new products, to show a production cost in their ex-ante and ex-post calculations that is higher than the real one (this is becoming the typical behaviour of enterprises in self-accounting systems).

Wherever the principles of the new economic system can be realised, "secrecy" gradually loses the functions which it serves in both the other types of system (though naturally this does not necessarily lead to their immediate termination), because now it is market relations that directly determine the prosperity of enterprise activity. At the same time, competition creates new types of enter-prise secrets which cause "news blackouts", especially on the fundamental questions of technical development. And if no effec-tive attempt is made to impose social supervision over this secrecy, generated by a rational point of view, then there will be almost nothing to stop the rise of the "castle" with its over-organisation and its peculiarly stifling atmosphere.

XI: The Intelligentsia and the Administration

The concept of the "intelligentsia" is under attack from many sides these days. The justification of its use is questioned from a variety of standpoints.

In first place amongst the rows of those doubting its usefulness stand those who adopt the "histmat" approach. If this approach is to remain consistent with its initial premises, at least when they are applied to socialism, it must reject the category of "intelligentsia". At a discussion held in the editorial office of the *Tarsadalmi Szemle* ("The Social Review") some two years ago, it was announced that it was now high time to dismiss the concept of the intelligentsia, since it had been rendered out-of-date by the course of social development.

At the same time the empirical approach cannot be content with this concept either. Its followers take the term to mean some form of statistical group, but argue that the basic criteria on which individual people could qualify for this classification are lacking. Fortunately, however, no one has yet worked out any such criteria, and so the empirical approach—quite justifiably, in terms of its own way of thinking—throws doubt on the validity of employing this term.

At the same time everyday language, and even the official language too, obstinately resists the scepticism of science and keeps repeating the term to the point of boredom. True, it is not used without ambiguity. Often it tends to be identified unreservedly with "brain workers", while on other occasions it is taken to such an extreme as to include only the most outstanding creative minds of our civilisation. It is even at times taken to mean an ethical type of behaviour. As a matter of fact this "mistake" was often made in the past by social science itself, at least while it continued to regard one of its tasks as being to provide some definition of the concept of the intelligentsia.

Which view should we adopt, then? The sceptical scientific approach, or that of both everyday and official language which regards the intelligentsia as a social reality, even if not one that can be treated with scientific exactitude?

In the following pages I shall try to prove that this latter approach, in spite of all its inexactness, grasps a very important aspect of our social reality, and does so better than the "scientific" approach referred to.

Starting from this conviction, I shall try to sketch out a conceptual definition of the intelligentsia, a definition that I find both possible and practical. I shall also try to outline the relationship of this social stratum to the administration, and to the bureaucracy as it is understood in the sociological meaning of the term. (I do not treat this latter expression in any pejorative way. I mean by "bureaucracy" apparatuses whose workers pursue their activities both as a vocation and as their principal occupation, and also with the appropriate expertise and competence.)

In trying to give a sociological definition of the intelligentsia, I think we should not set out to look for a group whose place in the structure of society can be precisely circumscribed, but should rather concentrate on the function which is implied by the term in its most widely-used everyday interpretation. (This function also explains the widespread usage of the term.) Terms without functions either rapidly drop out of everyday usage, or their contents pass through changes that lead to the emergence of new functions.

From this approach we can make use of a definition such as that used by Istvan Kardos in his doctoral dissertation on the question of the intelligentsia. He suggests that the tasks or functions of the intelligentsia should be seen as the creation of new intellectual values, or the application and communication of intellectual values in a creative way.

We have, of course, to admit that the two expressions used in this definition, that is "new intellectual values" and "application and communication in a creative way", are not objective categories, but depend upon the subjective judgement of what we mean by new intellectual values and the criterion "creative". The range of meaning of these expressions can vary, according to the value systems of different individuals, and science cannot produce definitions for them that would satisfy the requirements of precision demanded by the approach of empirical sociology.

However, this indisputable ambiguity and lack of definition does not mean that it is impossible for either of these expressions, that is "new intellectual values" and "application and communication in a creative manner", to be made understandable. It is easy to demonstrate that each of these expressions possesses a detectable, palpable and rational core, which enables us to widen or narrow down the meaning of the term. As a matter of fact we always come across similar problems whenever we attempt to

183

establish definitions of individual social classes or strata that are precise from the point of view of social science.

Practical experience proves convincingly that the creation of new intellectual values is a very important aspect of social development. Some outstanding men come to fulfil these functions; others however, for various social reasons, are unable to complete such tasks. It is indisputable that Aristotle, Dante, Archimedes, Marx, Newton, Einstein—and we could continue the list indefinitely—produced intellectual values such as the vast majority of their contemporaries were unable to produce, having neither the talent nor the social position which would have made this possible. It is also beyond doubt that, in the application and communication of values, it is also possible to distinguish the creative aspect from mechanical and merely routine activity, from the simple transmission and application of knowledge. Even if he does not produce new value in the true sense of the word, it is in this creative aspect that man recreates already existing intellectual values according to the requirements of particular circumstances or of his own value system, and in so doing enriches the civilisation of mankind. On this basis we can consider both the dedicated teacher or educator and the research engineer who designs a new technology or product to be members of the intelligentsia.

One can hardly dismiss the actual existence and social importance of the functions of the intelligentsia when interpreted in this way. It is perhaps unnecessary to point out that at the present stage of historical development, and for the foreseeable future, it will not be possible for all the members of society to develop their intellectual abilities to the same extent, and that therefore structural divisions will inevitably emerge. The intelligentsia exists whether we like it or not.

At the present stage of the division of labour in society, we can find occupations which require activity of the type performed by the intelligentsia in the sense just described, and men who—even irrespective of their occupation—either are or are not capable of fulfilling such tasks. In this respect it is certainly not true, as the old saying would have it, that "He who was given an office by God was given brains too". An intellectual job in itself does not make anybody into an intellectual.

One of the most important preconditions of social development is precisely the possibility for the activity of the intelligentsia to develop freely within the given limits imposed by the stage of social development. In other words, there should be opportunities for more and more people to become capable of doing such work, and their activity should be organically and effectively integrated, as far as possible, into the whole of social development.

In class societies this problem raises above all else the question of the extent to which the intelligentsia, and the activity produced by them, joins forces—directly or indirectly—with the classes and movements acting in the interests of social progress. In this question, which is a much debated one within marxism, there is a special importance in the relationship of the intelligentsia to the administrative apparatuses. The importance of these apparatuses is itself increasing, and particularly so in the socialist societies, where there are no class problems comparable with those of capitalist society.

From this viewpoint, we can witness in modern societies the emergence of a most unique contradiction. (a) On the one hand, the administration and management of society increasingly falls into the hands of hierarchically organised apparatuses (in sociology this is called bureaucratic management). For structural reasons and from different points of view, these can come into conflict with the functions of the intelligentsia, that is with their structural characteristics. (b) On the other hand, in contrast with previous societies, there is a much wider scope for the spreading and development of those functions which we have previously described as those of the intelligentsia. At the same time the activities which can be classified as those of the intelligentsia have also grown in strength and significance. However, on account of the first tendency, this indisputable development can nowhere lead to the management of society passing into the hands of the intelligentsia, even though many people have greatly cherished such an illusion. There is certainly no obvious tendency towards increased participation in power by the intelligentsia.

In order to understand the real nature of this contradiction, we need to study the typical attitudes of the administration towards the tasks of the intelligentsia. This can also explain their relation to the substratum of the intelligentsia in which these tasks and functions reach their development *par excellence.*

The guiding principle of the administrative apparatus is effectiveness, and in most cases this means the effectiveness of a particular institution and not that of social activity in general. It is virtually never identical with what is socially effective. The extent of synchronisation or asynchronisation depends mostly on the sort of macrostructure which the particular institution fits into, and on its specific function within that system.

It is in this sense that we can speak of the particular interest of

185

the institution (whether it be a state or a co-operative enterprise), with which the administrative apparatus necessarily identifies. And above all this is the very source of conflict between the apparatus and the intelligentsia, a conflict which arises from objective circumstances and structural causes.

Thus the interest of the members of the intelligentsia—to the extent that they really identify with their function—is related not to any particular institution, but to the special field of the creation, application and communication of intellectual values. In this way the particular interest of the intelligentsia is more easily raised to the level of the general interest. This of course does not rule out the possibility of particular individuals turning the general interest of the intelligentsia into a special aim of their own, one which would then come into conflict with the general interest. We could instance innumerable examples to prove this, from every field of science, art and education.

Grotesque situations often arise in history where the apparatuses which claim to represent the society as a whole, but which in fact have made an ideology of their own particular interests, come into conflict with a section of the intelligentsia. On the one hand, those sections of the intelligentsia who identify with their own particular functions, without being able to differentiate the general interest from their own particular interest, consider the general interest to be their own interest. On the other hand, the administration considers its own particular interest to be the general interest. But we can also come across other situations where groups of the intelligentsia claim to be representing the universality of intellectual values, when in fact they have become slaves to the particularism of their own specialist concerns, and when in opposition to them it is the administration that represents social interests of a higher order. It is enough just to think of certain fields of science which, in a small country like Hungary, seek to expand their activities within their national boundaries whatever the expense.

At the same time it follows that conflicts of interest between the administrative apparatus and various groups of the intelligentsia are likely to become most intense when the one or the other, or both at the same time, consider their own particular interest to be the general interest and refuse to allow even the slightest degree of tolerance.

The chief and perhaps most frequent source of conflict between the administration and the intelligentsia, a conflict which goes further than a mere clash of interests, arises from the hierarchial structure of the former. The intelligentsia is not against hierarchy in general; indeed, it itself often gives rise to a very strict hierarchy on the basis of its own system of values, a hierarchy within which the different substrata of the intelligentsia are very clearly differentiated. It is only that form of hierarchy which is based on official rank that the intelligentsia rejects.

Wherever the hierarchy of official rank comes into contact with the hierarchy based on the scale of values of different substrata of the intelligentsia (if they in fact meet anywhere at all) there will always be conflict between them. Individuals who appear important in one hierarchy will appear unimportant in the other, and vice-versa: unimportant people become important individuals in the eyes of different sets of people. In modern societies this conflict can only be moderated through the growth of mutual tolerance. However, neither of these groups has so far shown any particular propensity towards such tolerance.

Frequent conflicts also arise between the different types of criticism expressed by the administration and the intelligentsia. Expressing myself cautiously, I would argue that the administrative apparatuses are generally not prepared to look for the causes of obvious faults and shortcomings within the areas of their own activity. They generally prefer to attribute them to natural causes (bad weather, shortage of raw materials, etc.) or to the backwardness of the masses (e.g. by ideological arguments, such as that socialist consciousness lags behind developments in the objective sphere). Nor is it all that rare for them to blame the faults and shortcomings on the activity of the intelligentsia itself.

In contrast with this apologetic attitude, the intelligentsia often adopts a moralistic criticism, judging that which exists by comparing it with what they consider ought to be, according to the system of values which they hold. And they do all this without weighing the actual possibilities, and without choosing between these actual possibilities on the basis of their own system of values.

Thus two attitudes come into conflict: the apologetic one that mechanically defends the existing institutional order, and the moralistic one that completely fails to consider the actual alternatives, the much talked of "unconstructive" criticism.

As I am empirically quoting statistics to prove my thesis, the reader may well believe that I have got into some blind alley of abstraction. I would simply like to mention two cases, as examples which—even if they don't definitely prove my point of view—may at least make it to a large degree probable.

The first case is that of Tibor Zam, who wrote a criticism of the *Hortobagy* state farm which contained many noteworthy suggestions, but which gave rise to considerable anger and outright condemnation not only from the management of the state farm, but from the county authorities too. Another writer, the sociographer Antal Vegh, had similar experiences when his study of the village of Peneszlak aroused the indignation of the administrative apparatus of the neighbouring county. This conflict has been authentically depicted by Jozsef Darvas, who has written both an essay and a play about it.

Neither the intelligentsia nor the administration can be categorically classified as either good or bad, even though each often likes to categorise the other in this way. The intelligentsia is happy to adopt the pejorative picture of bureaucracy that is held by everyday opinion. Indeed, it is not at all reluctant to take an active part in promoting this view. Similarly, the administration frequently speaks of the intelligentsia as bohemian, good-for-nothing intellectuals who are isolated from the masses, and who act only as fetters on the efficient work of organisations.

At the same time, however, social development requires the development of both of these social groups and of the functions they perform. Although their functions are not always completely separate from each other, and although we can often witness a "personal union" between the roles of the intelligentsia and the administration, the social division of labour excludes the possibility of creating any meaningful harmony between them—at least for the foreseeable future. Consequently there is no other solution left apart from that of mutual tolerance, even though the ideologies created by the particular interests of the intelligentsia on the one hand, and the administration on the other, will brand this as opportunist.

Postscript: Twenty Years after Khrushchev's Secret Report

[The following text is of a letter sent by Andras Hegedus to the Bertrand Russell Peace Foundation on the occasion of the twentieth anniversary of Khrushchev's secret report to the Twentieth Congress of the CPSU in 1956.]

I cannot give a purely theoretical, objective answer to the question of the importance of this event; I can only give a subjective one, because on essential matters my attitudes to them have changed over the last twenty years.

At the time of the twentieth congress I had, as you probably know, an important role (as Prime Minister) in the stalinist power structure. This position, and the previous course of my life, determined to a large extent my attitudes towards the Congress documents. At that time, the main motive of my thoughts and acts was an anxiety, not so much for socialism (as I can see now in retrospect) as for the existing power structure. I considered these two elements as equivalent; at that time, in Hungary, I did not realise that it had become necessary, in the interests of socialist development, to fundamentally transform the power structure—not only in personal respects but in institutional ones too. All this made it impossible for me to recognise the real importance of the Congress. I understood it only during the years after 1956, when it became possible for me to think over the causes of the crisis of socialist development, above all in Hungary. I began to analyse social relationships in the East European countries, primarily in terms of their sociology, and step by step I began to turn against the apologetic official ideology. At about the time of the tenth anniversary of the Twentieth Congress I came to recognise the fact that self-analysis and self-criticism, on a marxist basis, had become a historical possibility and necessity in the East European countries. During my scientific work I came to the conviction that apologetics for the new social relations had become a real obstacle in the path of socialist development in these countries.

In the light of this conviction, I saw the Twentieth Congress then as a daring attempt to break with the apologetic ideology and its attitudes. At this time, in the mid-sixties, it seemed to me that the internal critique might gain ground in the marxist social sciences and so could contribute to the success of reforms initiated from above, and that this could therefore directly assist in developing social practice. In consequence, like the majority of my colleagues today, I was living in a special atmosphere of reformist

189

optimism.

The following decade failed to justify some of these expectations: the self-analysis and self-criticism of socialism have not asserted themselves, and the period of reforms was limited to a very short time. The internal critique struggled between the devil and the deep sea: on the one hand, anti-communism endeavoured (and still does) to profit from it for its own purposes, and on the other hand the official ideological apologists regarded and still regard it as an external, hostile critique, and they try to restrict it even by administrative measures.

All these things explain why, in recent years, the Twentieth Congress and especially Khrushchev's report have been less mentioned officially. But the reasons for the repression of internal criticism, in my view, are not to be sought primarily in the internal social and economic relations of East European countries, but rather in the peculiarities of today's world politics. The continuation of self-criticism and self-analysis is in the elementary interest both of these societies and of socialist thought, since the lack of it threatens the socialist perspective of these societies and their dynamism.

It would, however, be an illusion to expect a new period of reform in the near future. Thus we can observe an increase in social pessimism, and in the feeling that these societies have lost all their opportunities for developing towards socialist perspectives. I naturally understand the grounds for this pessimism, but I cannot agree with it. The initiative for reform and likewise the failure of reforms, have both resulted from activities taking place mainly in the upper levels of the power structure. But various movements are appearing among the masses, which I think are opening up more and more possibilities for the realisation of socialist values in everyday life, and these are very important for the perspectives of socialism.

A critical marxist social science cannot now deal with the most important macrostructural problems of these societies in the hope that it can improve social practice immediately. But such an analysis has, of course, a theoretical importance today; and it is now necessary and practically useful to analyse the changes in everyday life, with the aim of encouraging the development of movements pointing towards a socialist perspective. The direct and indirect influence of the Twentieth Congress is, I think, more effective and more irrevocable among the masses in their everyday life than it is in the area of politics or of the power structure.

Andras Hegedus, Budapest, 8 June, 1976.

Notes

1. Marx and Engels, *Complete Works*, vol. 8, p. 185 (Hungarian edition).
2. *Ibid.*, vol. 1, p. 187.
3. *Ibid.*, p. 251.
4. Rousseau, *The Social Contract*, Book 1, chapter 6.
5. Marx, *The Eighteenth Brumaire of Louis Bonaparte*, part 4.
6. Lenin, *State and Revolution*, chapter 6, part 3.
7. Lenin's letter to M. Sokolov, published in *Pravda* in January, 1924.
8. Marx, *Critique of Hegel's "Philosophy of Law"*, chapter 1, part B.
9. Published in *Valosag*, Budapest, March 1965.
10. Marx, *Critique of Hegel's "Philosophy of Law"* in Marx and Engels, *Collected Works*, vol. 3, p. 47 (English edition).
11. Sandor Szalai, "The Research of Research" in *Magyar Filozofiai Szemle*, 1965, p. 107 (in Hungarian).
12. S. L. Rubinshtein, *Osnovy obshcheï psikhologii*, Moscow, 1954.
13. Eugene Randsepp, *Manning Creative Scientists and Engineers*.
14. Veljko Rus, "Institutionalisation of the Revolutionary Movement" in *Praxis* (international edition) 1967, no. 2, p. 201.
15. *Vestnik Komm. Akademiï*, Moscow, 1924, vol. 9, p. 69.
16. S. Lozovsky, *Lenin i professional'noe dvizhenie*, Moscow, 1925, p. 23.
17. *Narodnoe khozyaïstvo*, Moscow, Jan.-Feb. 1921, p. 15.
18. *Ibid.*, p. 19.
19. E. Preobrazhensky, *Anarkhizm i kommunism*, Moscow, 1921 (revised edition).
20. S. Lozovsky in *Narodnoe khozyaïstvo*, 1922, no. 8, pp. 50-1.
21. N. Bukharin, "NEP i professional'nie soyuzy" in *Vestnik agitatsii i propagandy*, nd.
22. Lenin, *Collected Works*, vol. 32, p. 4.
23. *Kommunisticheskoe khozyvaïstvo*, Jan.-Feb. 1921, p. 15.
24. *Izvestia raboche-krestyanskoï inspektsii*, Moscow, 1920, no. 2, p. 1.
25. *Ibid.*, 1920, no. 3, p. 2.
26. See *Voprosi agitatsii i propagandy*, Jan. 1922.
27. *Ibid.*, pp., 33-4.
28. *Ibid.* 1921, no. 9-10, p. 39.
29. See J. Stalin, *Questions of Leninism*.
30. Rezso Nyers, "The Probable Social and Political Effects of the New Economic System" in *Tarsadalmi Szemle*, 1968, no. 3 (in Hungarian).
31. See Oskar Lange, *Political Economy*.
32. See *ibid.*
33. See Marx, *Moralising Critique and Critical Morals*.
34. See *ibid.*
35. Enrico Berlinguer, at the Tenth Congress of the Italian Communist Party.
36. Istvan Gergely, *Business Policy and Market Decisions of Capitalist Enterprises*, Budapest 1969 (in Hungarian).
37. L. Kritsman, *Geroicheskii period velikoi russkoi revolyutsii*, Moscow, 1924, p. 94.

38. *Ibid.*, p. 44.
39. Lenin, *Collected Works*, vol. 27, p. 148.
40. *Ibid.*, pp. 215-17.
41. *Narodnoe khozyaïstvo,* June-July 1921, p. 17.
42. *Ibid.*, January 1922.
43. *Krasnaya nov'*, November 1921, p. 191.
44. *Ibid.*
45. *Narodnoe khozyaïstvo,* 1921, no. 10, p. 7.
46. *Ibid.*, 1922, no. 4, p. 12.
47. *Ibid.*, 1920, no. 9-10, p. 5.
48. Isaac Deutscher, *The Prophet Armed,* vol. 1, pp. 509-10.
49. M. I. Tugan-Baranovsky, *Sotsialnie osnovy kooperatsii,* Moscow, 1918.
50. Lenin, *Collected Works,* vol. 30, p. 428.
51. *Ibid.*, vol. 27, p. 350.
52. *Krasnaya nov'*, November 1921, p. 140.
53. *Vestnik sotsialisticheskoï akademii,* 1924, Book 9, p. 80.
54. Lenin, *Collected Works,* vol. 33, p. 368.
55. *Ibid.*, vol. 30, pp. 309-10.
56. Marx, "Critical Marginal Notes on the Article 'The King of Prussia and Social Reform'" in Marx and Engels, *Collected Works,* vol. 3, p. 198.
57. R. K. Merton, *Bureaucratic Structure and Personality,* 1940.
58. Marx, "Contribution to the Critique of Hegel's 'Philosophy of Law'" in Marx and Engels, *Collected Works,* vol. 3, p. 46.
59. R. L. Simpson, "Vertical and Horizontal Communication in Formal Organisations" in *Administrative Science Quarterly,* 1959, no. 4.
60. W. H. Whyte, *The Organisation Man,* London, 1960, p. 8.
61. Agnes Heller, *The sociology of morality or the morality of sociology,* Budapest, 1964, pp. 66-7 (in Hungarian).

Index

193

Some other titles in the MOTIVE series

Michel Raptis
Revolution and Counter-Revolution in Chile

Henri Lefebyre
The Survival of Capitalism

Franz Jakubowski
Ideology and Superstructure in Historical Materialism

Jiri Pelikan
Socialist Opposition in Eastern Europe

Agnes Heller
The Theory of Need in Marx

Mihaly Vajda
Fascism as a Mass Movement

Hilda Scott
Women and Socialism—Experiences from Eastern Europe

Andras Hegedus, Agnes Heller, Maria Markus, Mihaly Vajda
The Humanisation of Socialism

Bill Lomax
Hungary 1956

Henri Laborit
Decoding the Human Message